W0043038

LEADERSHIP BY PROXY

Poonam Barua has done something that I think few writers have been able to accomplish. She has provided her readers with a volume that has universal interest as it discusses major global issues involving women in the corporate sector. At the same time, the book is clearly rooted in the Indian experience and the volume is uniquely Indian.

Prof. Beryl Radin, *Public Policy Institute, Georgetown University and Editor, Georgetown University Press Book Series*

'Leadership by Proxy – The Story of Women in Corporate India' is a pioneer in its space and lays the foundation for businesses who believe in balanced leadership and gender inclusive growth.

The Book bravely paves the way for women to move from corporate hallways to boardrooms by presenting a compelling case for rejecting homogenous corporate boards as a way for business to grow and mature. With its personal narrative, compelling case studies and anecdotes, the book perfectly captures the journey of women in corporate India as they progressively find their voices and redefine boardroom rules, gender sensitive leadership and team dynamics.

I strongly believe that the future of businesses will lie in the way they view gender inclusion for their own economic benefit. Values such as respecting gender-based differences will not just drive innovation for business but will also play a strong role in the progress of the society as a whole.

Richard Rekhy, *Chief Executive Officer, KPMG*

Poonam Barua's new book is a clearly written and well-informed discussion of the most important challenge facing Indian businesses today.

This is a must read for every business leader that wants to re-look at the way they understand balanced leadership. *It is time* *for Corporate India to move from anecdotal evidence to compelling and rigorous economic measurement and Poonam's hard-hitting personal narrative style helps immensely!*

Raj Raghavan, *Head of Human Resources – Amazon India.*

Poonam Barua has led the dedicated and pioneering work done in India to create an ecosystem for women to serve on Boards.

With a zeal and enthusiasm that can only come from a very deeply felt connect, Poonam Barua has woven this seminal book which will be like a shining light for all engaged in corporate Boards related work.

India is emerging as a Governance Capital of the world and so this work has an International appeal.

Shailesh Haribhakti, *Chairman, Haribhakti LLP*

This book is the story of the efforts by Poonam Barua to create women leaders in corporate India, at a time when such leaders were few, inspired by the belief that India could only progress when 50% of the population got their share of leadership positions on merit, in an open transparent corporate culture. Of course reality was much different with the odds against women in their leadership journey. Poonam inspired a large number of women executives to work hard to reach the top, aspire for leadership positions, prove their worth against established belief that this aspiration was ahead of its time. All her extraordinary efforts seemed to have paid off with many corporates creating a more inclusive culture at the Board and other levels, to allow greater opportunities for women to rise to the top levels on their own merit.

T.V. Mohandas PAI, Chairman, Aarin Capital Partners.

LEADERSHIP BY PROXY

The Story of Women in Corporate India

POONAM BARUA

BLOOMSBURY
NEW DELHI • LONDON • OXFORD • NEW YORK • SYDNEY

First published in India 2015

© 2015 by Poonam Barua

All rights reserved. No part of this publication may be reproduced or
transmitted in any form or by any means, electronic or mechanical, including
photocopying, recording, or any information storage or retrieval system, without prior
permission in writing from the publishers.

No responsibility for loss caused to any individual or organization acting on or
refraining from action as a result of the material in this publication can be
accepted by Bloomsbury or the author.

The content of this book is the sole expression and opinion of its author.
The publisher in no manner is liable for any opinion or views
expressed by the author. While best efforts have been made in preparing this
book, the publisher makes no representations or warranties of any kind and
assumes no liabilities of any kind with respect to the accuracy or completeness
of the content and specifically disclaims any implied warranties of
merchantability or fitness of use for a particular purpose.

The publisher believes that the content of this book does not violate any
existing copyright/intellectual property of others in any manner whatsoever.
However, in case any source has not been duly attributed, the publisher may
be notified in writing for necessary action.

BLOOMSBURY and the Diana logo are trademarks of Bloomsbury Publishing Plc

ISBN 978 93 854 3635 2
2 4 6 8 10 9 7 5 3 1

Bloomsbury Publishing India Pvt. Ltd
DDA Complex, LSC Building No.4
Second Floor, Pocket C – 6 & 7, Vasant Kunj
New Delhi 110070
www.bloomsbury.com

Typeset by Manmohan Kumar
Printed and bound in India by Thomson Press India Ltd.

To find out more about our authors and books visit www.bloomsbury.com.
Here you will find extracts, author interviews, details of forthcoming
events and the option to sign up for our newsletters.

Notes:

*This book is dedicated to the 500 million women of India –
and my courageous mother, Shakuntala*

*With warm appreciation to my dear son Bacchus Barua –
on whose small kitchen table this book was written in 45 days,
overlooking the misty Grouse Mountain in Vancouver –
pushing his mother to cross the limits of star-shine*

*To my husband Shankar Barua – who has taught me the
meaning of being truly "free".....*

CONTENTS

Foreword: N.R. Narayana Murthy, Founder – Infosys Limited   xi

Prologue: "I am the Storm in the Tea cup"   xiii

1. Seeding the Mission: For Women in Leadership   1

2. Passions of the Mind: From Wall Street in Manhattan to Dalal Street in Mumbai: The Fallacy of Unconscious Bias   15

3. In Pursuit of Balanced Leadership Womenomics: The Compelling Case for Women and Wealth-Creation   36

4. The Gender Context of Leadership: Talent is Universal – Opportunity is Not!   44

5. User's Guide to Mentoring: Lessons from celebrating 650 WILL Mentees in Corporate India   64

6. Validate and Verify! Benchmarking Best Employers for Women Companies   88

7. #It's my time now! The Golden voices of Indian Women Professionals   101

8. In Pursuit of Balanced Leadership: 50 Best Practices for Women in the Workplace   115

9. Retaining Women in the Workplace   128
   The Myth of Work-Life Balance

10. All Male Boards: Is there a Trust-Deficit for   142
    Women Board Directors?

11. Balanced Boards for Good Governance   161
    Diverse, Inclusive, Balanced, Sustainable
    & Resilient

12. Building Sensitive, Sustainable, and Sensible   175
    Organisations: Reverse Mentoring of Male Managers

13. "Soul-Sisters": You will find them everywhere! 185

14. Talking a walk down Mumbai's "red-light" area   189

ANNEXURE:

a) WILL Mother's Handbook;   195
   50 Best Practices for New and Entrant Mothers

b) WILL Balanced Leadership Value Model: 210
   Quantifying the Value of Women to Business

c) Testing the Waters   218
   For Women on Boards

About the Author   239

FOREWORD

"Leadership by Proxy" by Poonam Barua is a thought-provoking book that paves the way for creating a change in the approach of thinking of corporate India. The book puts forward best practices in the workplace that will support diverse corporate entities as a fundamental economic function to bring optimum rewards to business growth and societal progress.

This book is also a tribute to the 500 million women in India – who are contributing their time, talent, skills, value, knowledge and dedication to make an honest contribution to enhancing business performance and improving the society in which we live, and to nation-building. Without the contribution of these women, India will find it difficult to grow the economy and increase the prosperity of its citizens.

There is growing evidence amongst the Fortune 500 companies, that diversity can become a critical tool for innovation and competitive edge, and this book highlights the need to put policies and mentoring programs in place to support that. Such initiatives could help improve the participation of women in senior management and board roles in corporate India which is currently around 5–10% and is much lower than the 25–30% participation of their counterparts in Europe & North America.

The insights and perspectives in this book have been gathered from 7 years of hard and dedicated work of the *Forum for Women in Leadership* (WILL Forum). This forum was launched in November 2007 at the Infosys' boardroom with a mission and vision for creating opportunities and a larger role for women for progressive national and corporate development. Today, the WILL Forum is inspiring thousands of women across India and the world, to aspire for better careers and better incomes and has over 650 WILL Mentees across reputed companies in India and multinationals. This is likely to provide a rich and robust pipeline of women leaders for the next phase of corporate growth.

The book has an interesting narrative. It has compelling corporate anecdotes and case studies with real data on how women are progressively finding their voices in an evolving corporate world and are collectively redefining gender-sensitive leadership to aspire for board positions.

"Leadership by Proxy" is a book that beckons all stakeholders worldwide to bring meritorious leadership to the workplace, and find harmony, courtesy and dignity without the barriers of genders, nationalities, races and religious beliefs.

N.R. Narayana Murthy
Founder, Infosys Limited

PROLOGUE

'It is because I want to protect you from suffering such as I had to endure in my youth

Because my temperament and ideas were different – they are different,

From what the world accepts and understands,

That I tried to guide you…

Remember ……..

Nothing in your speech or action should cause the progress of Indian women to suffer; nothing in yourself should give room for wretched reactionary slave-minds to say

"This comes of giving too much education and freedom to our women."

Think over it my darling. Be great my little child….'

…… 1947. Sarojini Naidu, first women President of the Indian National Congress, and Indian Independence activist, in a letter to her daughter

There is an electrifying sense of high energy, aspirations, inspiration, bonding, ideas, contribution, commitment, courage, dialogue and goodwill – when 500 million women of India come together to share their voices and their vision. And, there is also a deep sense of despair, struggle, sacrifice, rejection, and resignation – about the wisdom of those who have dominated the hallways of power for hundreds of years in the societies, communities, and the world where we live.

It is almost baffling to understand how the majority of valuable, hardworking and high delivering women of India – who constitute 50% of the one billion Indian population and 8% of the total world population – have been relegated to the lowest levels of workspaces and side-lined in the decision-making strategies, defined narrowly by conservative hierarchies of linear leadership of male-dominated networks that allow little space for colours of diversity, individuality, and "different strokes" – which are the hallmark of creativity, innovation, and competitive excellence.

There are innumerable stories being told by smart corporate women – of their accomplishments and conflicts, of compromise with dignity and compassion, of sacrifices aimed at protecting their loved ones, and of courage that kept them empowered – in an unequal eco-system that is unable to "recognise, reward, and respect" different sensibilities and perceives leadership only in the limited sense of its own boundaries.

It is time for corporate India to pay a tribute to these half-billion women in India – who are contributing their time, talent, skills, value, knowledge and dedication to make an honest contribution to enhancing business performance and improving the society in which we live and to nation-building. Without the value and skills of these women, India will find it difficult to attain and sustain its GDP growth rate on a high trajectory, that is being promised in the hallways of the World Economic Forum and build sustainable wealth-creation that is so critical for an emerging market like India – that constitutes 16% of the world population but only 6% of the world economy.

This book is aimed at giving "voice, visibility, and validation" to the aspirations of women for playing an important, substantive and leadership role in the corporate dynamics – and providing good governance as board directors, business leaders, and strategic decision-makers – that are presently dominated by outdated systems of recognizing high performers, and traditional board-room dynamics where there is little place for women "at the top," and the few women who make it – will remain a singular minority accounting for 5% of board directors and 10% of senior management in India.

This book is an archive of the stories, insights and experience sharing, with over 6,000 women across functions and companies in India and multinationals – that seeks to ensure that their voices will be heard in the corridors of best practice companies, that will provide them a level-playing field with dignity and equality.

The book is also a call to every CEO, HR leader, Board Director, and top-management – to get past their comfort-zones of leadership and recognise the damaging "opportunity- cost" of working at sub-optimal free markets – where women are the "least used resource in the world" and the future markets and consumption chains will pressure them to include women as partners, colleagues, and co-workers for best business results.

Business in India attends to this vast domain of women executives after all other business priorities have been attended to – like profits, corporate governance, risk, compensation – without recognizing that it is time to move from the "vicious-cycle to the virtuous-cycle", for long-term sustainability of all business and its stakeholders.

There is still time and hope to "reset the compass" for corporate India to become an "authentic" leader– in pursuit of "balanced and inclusive leadership" – in the years to come, and dismantle the present structure that will be unsustainable in the volatility of the dynamics of geo-politics and pressure for good corporate governance that gives mindfulness to the aspirations of all its stakeholders who comprise the societies and communities in which we live.

Most of all – it is time to hear the voices of the half-a-billion Indian women – who present an electrifying source of energy, vitality, talent, knowledge and intuitive skills and strategy – and who remain invisible and forgotten in the workplace, with few roadmaps to optimize their leadership qualities and aspirations.

It is time to get past the power-play – of Leadership by Proxy.

"I AM THE STORM IN THE TEA CUP"

Do you have a story?

What motivated you to start the WILL Forum mission for women in leadership?

What was the trigger and inspiration?

Do you have any mentors or sponsors who helped you to achieve this position?

I have been asked these questions several times, by several people all over the world – and often wonder at the "element" of the question itself:

I have no story to tell

There is no motivation or trigger

I have no mentors or sponsors

I do not know any inspiration

When a good job needs to be done – you just get up and do it

You do not need a story to start

The compelling outcome of the job in front of you – is your one and only motivation

Sponsors and mentors are "proxies" who will dilute the power of your own self –

Everyone has the Power of Self – you just have to find it & unleash it –

In a systematic, strategic, substantive, sensible, and stunning way –

And, you have to be your own Inspiration

Without any barriers
Without any negatives
Without any helping hands
Without any proxy
Without any stories

With distinction
With accomplishment
With stature
With courage & conviction
With seeing the "end" of the story even before you have started it
With single purpose and meaningfulness
With passion and persuasion
With substance and style
With Voice and Visibility

And with never taking "no" for an answer – unless you know it is physically and mentally impossible – being beyond the realms of our existing known universe and the lovely milky way-galaxy, billions of light years away in unknown spaces and domains

Leadership cannot be done by Proxy

Leadership has to be authentic and real

And all we need around us – are people who will "keep the faith"

The rest is called "clutter"
Time to get rid of the "noise" around you
And find your true-self

You have to be your own Inspiration
You have to be your own Energy
Or else – It will not work

Poonam Barua

SEEDING THE MISSION
For Women in Leadership

1

"The things that will destroy us are:
Politics without principle;
Pleasure without conscience;
Wealth without work;
Knowledge without character;
Business without morality;
Science without humanity;
And worship without sacrifice."

…Mahatma Gandhi

The mission and legacy for leadership are never started in a vacuum.
The seeds have to be rich, hungry, fertile, steadfast, and most of all determined to survive against all odds of human and nature's unpredictable behaviours.

Year, 2007: Bangalore

It was the summer of 2007 when I went to meet the distinguished N.R. Narayana Murthy, Founder and Chairman of Infosys Technologies, one of India's most admired IT company with revenues of over $8.7 billion located at the outskirts of

Bangalore– and who is one the finest pioneers of enterprise and wealth-creation, as defined by Adam Smith's "invisible hand" of competitive economics. I shared with Mr. Murthy – as a student would plead with their guide and mentor – my deep sense of dismay with the lack of women as visible and critical stakeholders in the fast emerging growth story of corporate India, and the economic loss of potential wealth, value, talent, strategy, and energy – to national progress and development. Mr Murthy's modest office is literally the smallest building in the sprawling forty-three acres of the Infosys campus – filled with green trees and plants, huge cutting-edge architecture buildings, state of the art media studio, polo-golf carts that take guests around the campus, and average- age 25 year-old young executives working at solutions-technology, building a bustling sense of energy at the Bangalore location. Also present at the meeting, was Mohan Das Pai, one of the finest corporate governance experts of volatile global markets – whose net worth can be measured as much by the billions of dollars of stocks he owns, as his commitment to social communities, which is the "one million children he feeds everyday" through his NGO work.

At the landmark Infosys campus that speaks volumes of the pioneering stories of how Indian software companies made a "footprint" in the world of global information technology, and how a non-existent company became the "IT bellwether" after getting listed at Nasdaq in less than a decade – I began my struggle to inspire and persuade the two legendary Directors from Infosys that it was critical to open a candid and substantive dialogue with the over 250 million women professionals of India – who so far had no networks, forums, or platforms to come together across industry, and share their aspirations, challenges, roadmaps, and distinctions – for national progress and sustainable growth. Infosys readily agreed to become our most gracious meeting host –

and we invited over 200 CEOs from Indian companies and multinationals to nominate their senior most women executives to discuss the roadmap for advancing women, understanding their perspectives, and leveraging the vast talent-pool of 500 million women, who rarely find a "voice" in the elite corridors of power in corporate India. What we got – were 40 participant nominations – ranging from a junior woman mechanic-engineer in one of India's largest automobile factories at Hosur (a small district outside of Bangalore), to a woman nominee who was the Executive Director of Tata Tea.

The discussions at the iconic Infosys Boardroom in the Fall of 2007 were the start of a visionary agenda to set a clear mandate for launching a "forum for women in leadership" – that will be owned by the women, and will dedicate itself to promoting the mission for advancing women and opening their world of opportunities. However, it was almost uncanny to hear the 40 women from across industry, speak in similar tones and similar voices about their workplace challenges – embedded in the lack of career clarity, low respect and support for women who raise families, lack of sensitivity to the gender style of working women, threat perceptions from competitive women, and a constant reminder of the "social-cultural- stereotypes" that the women's "place is in the home and family" that was impeding with their delivery and performance at work, at home, and as productive individuals. The robust and sometimes very personal discussions in the Infosys boardroom were also a sharp indictor of the volume of work that needed to be done – in raising the aspiration-levels of the 40% of women who form the fabric of business India, and who have been fed upon recycled role models of women who successfully 'balance home and family' – as if this was a Rubik-cube that would never see the same set of colours on one side – or women who would never see anyone who looked like them walking the elite hallways of corporate boardrooms, as if they were an ivory tower where women were rarely to be seen.

This was a true "slice" of the *forgotten* women of corporate India – who had no one to raise their levels of aspirations, visibility, role and functions, and acknowledge their leadership contributions. This is what had become of our women engineers, MBA's, communications experts, and business operations masters – who were relegated to working in sectors ranging from manufacturing to IT-solutions that were dominated by male stereotypes, patronizing attitudes about women and families- care and lack of a clear roadmap for moving women into strategic decision-making positions in the organization, in an unequal playing field where "recognition, risk, and reward" were not correlations of the same mathematical equation.

Women: The Invisible Heroes of India's Growth Story

If there was ever a good case-study of how leadership by proxy works – the women of corporate India seemed to be the invisible heroes of India's leadership growth story.

There also seems to be universality about this experience worldwide – among the talented, hardworking, and accomplished women across continents, geographies, cultures, and professions – who have spoken about gender-discrimination in business and the workplace with continuing pressure on women to work "harder, stronger, faster – on the same field."

From where we stand today, there are 500 million women in India, who constitute half of India's over 1.2 billion population that comprises of multiple and complex diverse, ethnic, religious, and cultural sub-groups that form part of the Indian democratic sub-continent.

Further, the 500 million Indian women alone constitute 8%

of the total world population, which is a powerful economic force with immense "potential and promise" for influencing the sustainability and wealth-creation of this planet – and is also significantly higher than many large developing countries' percentage of the world population.

From a demographic point of view, the 500 million Indian women are nearly double the entire population of the United States, and about 250 million Indian women are below the age of 30 years – and they are energetic, with basic education and skills, and many are logged into the successor-generation phenomena of mobile phones, internet, and social media. They also constitute a fast-growing $12 trillion dollar consumer global market ready with "consumer-delight backed by disposable income" for almost every commodity available – from household goods to automobiles to leisure wellness. They also represent a large potential saving and investor fund, that goes unutilized due to lack of attention on women as key investors and suppliers, constituting less than 20% of the Indian mutual funds and financial instruments markets in India.

In spite of this staggering volume of economic and business potential, presently women account for less than 5% of corporate board director positions in India and less than 10% of senior management in the over 6,000 companies listed on the Bombay Stock Exchange. This is one of the lowest in the world, as compared to countries like Europe and USA, where women account for nearly 25–30% of senior management positions and 18–40% of board directors positions. To explain these dismal numbers on account of the "socio-economic- cultural" environment in India, or the lack of qualified women in a "meritocracy- based" corporate system – would be doing injustice to the vast volume of women's expectations and aspirations who are ready to take front-line jobs for advancing their careers, and are fully qualified on performance and delivery – given an equal opportunity meritocracy based eco-system of business and professional ethics.

As an economist, who has spent my entire rigour of academia at the Delhi School of Economics, being educated by stellar professors on how business entities can maximize wealth and value creation under a robust capitalist economy – I remain mystified that women are still the least used resource in the world– and why this is just plain bad economics, that continues to keep the world at a sub-optimal growth trajectory.

As the onslaught of rapid technology, volatile geopolitics, unprecedented pace of artificial intelligence and social media and the wide cultural shifts takes place around the world – it is becoming clear that no business leadership story will be complete for any sector or industry, that does not leverage the vast talent pool and economic productivity of the women stakeholders. *"New Age economics"* will compel companies to exhibit new work cultures, new formats of doing business, focus on vast and diverse stakeholders, engage with markets that have no defined frontiers for consumers who make their discretionary "choices", where social media has dismantled hierarchical power structures empowering the individual, and where employees work in flexible spaces and flexible timelines. Worldwide, there is a compelling trend towards creating "global, diverse, and inclusive" companies – where the "leadership styles of yesterday" will not be the successful "leadership styles of tomorrow." Every stakeholder will be looking for a picture that defines their own "mirror" in the shape of the new age companies – and each stakeholder's contribution will become critical to the survival of businesses in a highly competitive, cutting-edge marketplace – *where long-term sustainability and inclusive growth have become the hallmarks of success.*

We are looking at a paradigm shift of leadership – and it plays naturally to the strengths of women. The tide has turned. The leadership skills that come naturally to women are now absolutely necessary for companies to thrive. So much of what it takes to be a leader has been historically defined by men. Women are beginning to create a compelling need to redefining how boardrooms, companies, and management view their talents, markets, and stakeholder value creation.

To bring sharp definition to the unique style of women in leadership, we released the *WILL- KPMG Report on "Differentiating Styles of Women in Leadership"* (2010) that focused for the first time on how women bring distinct personality and motivational strengths to leadership. They have an open, collegial, and consensus-building approach to business – that is less likely to be found in male executives who are more inclined towards linear and ambitious approach to their jobs and careers. Women seem to be totally "ahead of the curve", showing signs of being assertive, persuasive, emphatic, willing to take risks, outgoing, and with a need to "get things done". These personality qualities combine to create a leadership profile that is much more conducive to today's diverse workplace – where information is shared freely, collaboration is vital, and good teamwork distinguishes the best companies.

So, what will "New Age Companies" with "balanced leadership" and inclusive-growth – that have a visible and substantive component of women's leadership skills on strategic decision making – look like?

In fact, the term "New Age companies" was first heard at the 3rd WILL USA Conference hosted by Thomson Reuters, in the heart of bustling, creative and innovative Times Square in New York, in the Fall of 2013. With a group of dedicated CEOs, senior managers, business heads, and diversity thought-leaders – from best performing companies including Tata Consultancy Services, KPMG, General Electric, MSD Pharma, Capgemini,

JP Morgan, Credit Suisse, Deloitte Consulting, McGraw Hill, Wipro Technologies, Goldman Sachs, Bloomberg, John Deere, Financial Women's Association, Families and Works Institute – it was in many ways a "watershed" moment, taking the entire debate on balanced leadership to a whole new level that would "weave" diversity, good governance, equal opportunity, and innovation into a new corporate culture, where balanced boards would be the natural custodians of inclusive growth and global leadership.

In an environment where pressures to perform are relentless and there are unprecedented expectations from the diverse range of stakeholders, customers, supplier, employees, and business nationalities – there was a clear consensus that firms need to move "from command and control" leadership to a collaborative strategy, implying more opportunity for **each individual** *to contribute to the business performance and common good as a full custodian.*

This is the real essence of the need for respecting diversity and individual value in the "new-age companies", where "wealth creation" is being defined in unique ways, driven by a business world that is becoming increasingly virtual.

It is also important that the "tone is clearly set from the top" and the company board embraces the agenda for corporate culture change – so that the transition to balanced leadership can be faster, deeper, and will bring better rewards for doing business.

These will be companies that will prepare for transition to corporate cultures that are more receptive across nationalities, geographies, gender, ethnic groups, and all minorities. They will celebrate the "individual" values without bias; with structured mentoring of executives across all levels of the organization to embrace the change. Businesses will start celebrating "new-age role models" – who will break the traditional mould of successful business leaders and define ways that adapt a collaborative work ethic, respect for families and colleagues, dispense with command

and control hierarchies, and embrace diversity in all its respects.

New Age companies will also be fast putting into place "enabling policies", targeted programs for equal opportunity in the workplace and advancement of women, and increasing the pipeline for all stakeholders at the mid-level and entry level, to nurture "balanced boards" that will be the custodians of good governance and smart economics at the top-end of the scale. New Age companies will go beyond the traditional definition of "talent pool" as articulated by HR experts over the past decades – to giving a truly global and innovative mindset to the organization. Companies will be fast leveraging the rate of change of technology, for unleashing a "new breed" of the millennium generation, new hiring practices, engagement, and unexplored but reliable retention strategies.

As early as 2010, a similar definition of "balanced leadership" came up when John **Flannery**, the then CEO of GE India, was chairing the 13*th* *WILL Forum India* meeting, with a group of senior women executives from across leading multinationals that crowd the high –rise spaces of Gurgaon, and the extended national capital region of New Delhi. The discussion emphasis kept moving towards the demonstrated strengths of women over the years, that has provided the critical "tail-wind" to propel the front-line business leadership growth – that remains visibly dominated only by male managers, business units heads, and CXOs – who seem to take all the credit for the exponential growth of Indian software industries, BPOs, banking and finance, and core manufacturing particularly in renewable energy and power, cement and steel, and pharmaceutical industry. *(Refer WILL Report: In Pursuit of Balanced Leadership, 2011)*

Escalating the Dialogue for Women:
From Talent and HR – to Good Governance and Risk
From Empowering Women – to Advancing Women

There is a compelling need to escalate the dialogue for women in leadership across the business world, and particularly in corporate India – from the elementary discussions of "HR policies and talent retention" to focus on "good governance and risk management", where the CEO and Corporate Boards become the custodians of commitment to building global & diverse organizations – as a critical enterprise risk management priority.

As the non-financial risks of volatile geo-politics, reputation risk of companies, intellectual property, and environmental impacts become important for boardroom agendas – companies will have to find experts beyond the traditional auditors, board directors who are on several Boards at one time, and powerful ex-bureaucrats – and look for people who understand sustainable development, community care, and public spiritedness in addition to good business strategy.

With 70% of Indian businesses being owner–promoter driven, good corporate governance is a new and compliance based best practice in corporate India – that became embedded with the setting up in 1992 of the Securities and Exchanges Board of India (SEBI) that was vested with the legal and regulatory framework and authority, to replace the outdated and ineffective Indian Companies Act of 1956. But it was only in 2005, that terms like *shareholder activism, stakeholder sustainability, shareholder market value, enterprise risk management, corporate governance* became known to Indian businesses. These terms were not easily embraced for many years by Indian CEOs and boardrooms – with seeming disregard about the correlation between good governance and profits, innovation and competitive economics, long-term vs. short-termism, *and excessive reliance on "talent and people" with little attention to "inclusive talent and diversity of people".*

One of the few real believers and pioneers of the power of good corporate governance was Dr J.J. Irani, one of the most successful icon CEOs of Tata Steel, and a Member of the Board of the over

USD 130.billion Tata Sons Group – and one of the finest human beings, CEO, and corporate visionaries that India has produced. Having watched him closely for many years – his demeanour betrays his deep understanding of the vast range of "communities" and the men, women and children, that actually make up the "corporate entity" that Joseph Schumpeter defined in the early 1900s – and his firm inclination to say "no" to any practice where due diligence, transparency, trust, and corporate governance were at risk. When asked why the Tata Board had no women – he promptly said that he did not see any women at the Tata Group who were visible, articulate, made their executive presence, and contributed substantively to the debates and discussions on stakeholder value creation. This was an eye-opening statement – *that the women were not only being not heard in corporate India – they were also not visible!*

These high-powered networks that surround corporate India – are as difficult to penetrate for the women as in other parts of the world. What distinguishes the workplace in India, is that the power networks that business men have built over the years, has created a fire-wall of close relationships between mid-level and senior level managers across industry that appears to be choking innovative thinking, bright ideas and fresh perspectives – and instead places power in the hands of those who are self-styled leaders with little interest in building *authentic leadership*. The 40% women executives of corporate India are the worst affected by this, as they are unable to devote time to cracking these male networks, and since only 8% women are in senior management they have no way to compete with an alternative power network that will be as influential and high on delivery.

It's not about D&I (Diversity & Inclusivity) – It's about DNA!

It's about the heart, and the mind, and spirit – is the "mindset" ready to embrace inclusive growth?

The world is now witnessing a powerful and irreversible move among companies worldwide to "empower" women through the "diversity and inclusivity" initiatives, which is the "right move in the right direction" – but only when it is handled with the right "moral compass" and with "gender-auditing capability practices" well embedded in the organization. Otherwise, the translation of this excellent cultural evolution in India seems to have only invested more power in the hands of the HR leaders, who have now relegated women-related-policies to another "talent bucket issue" that remains at the bottom of the corporate ladder, and not a strategic tool of business investment and growth strategy. I have often witnessed presentations by leading companies on their D&I initiatives that cover every aspect of women's employee development – from basic nurturing women, to building women networks, to mentoring women – but the last slide for the policies taken for *"advancing women"* in the organization is often missing.

It is therefore no surprise, that "on an average" – the top performing blue-chip companies in India today listed on the Bombay Stock Exchange – shows the following dismal statistics:

Average number of women at the entry level is 50%; at the mid-level is 40%, and at the top-band of the executive leadership the number of women is as low as between 1–10%. In fact, it is hard to find companies in India that have more than 10% women in the top-level – and most of them are still struggling with low percentage levels of between 5–8%.

This declining percentage of women at the top-levels cannot be explained away by the slow-down in women's careers, and lack of women' s talent – as the number of women who leave the workforce on account of "family responsibilities" could be no more than 12–15% – and that too among women below the age of thirty-five. Also, the current popular practice of launching company initiatives to "bringing women back to work" or "second-career women" –does nothing to advancing the careers of these women – except give them "a professional employment". *'The reality is that a large part of the declining women at the top-brackets of company leadership is a clear reflection on the lack of equal opportunity and fair-promotions at the top-end of the business unit – that keeps most of the women in the "mid-level" for almost their entire careers in the organization.'* My dear friend Aruna Newton, Learning and Diversity Leader of Infosys Technologies, and also the first Woman President of the Electronics Association of Bangalore – refers to this as, "The large underbelly of women executives in corporate India that needs to be urgently attended to, to enhance the appetite for creativity and innovation particularly in the tech-and-software industry."

On the flip side – companies which display a large number of women at the top levels of about 11– 15% in corporate India and appear to be doing well on promoting women in the workplace – are often showing less than 20% women in their total workforce! This is a clear indicator of an empty leadership pipeline of women – with companies "transplanting" women in the top-level brackets after recruiting from other companies, which is more of a "window-dressing" for pacifying investors and shareholders – rather than building a robust and strong "women in leadership" agenda for the company.

This is where we begin our journey in this book– to understand how world class companies aspire to do business in world class global markets, and create irresistible value-addition – and at the same time have no validation of commitment to include the women in their strategic leadership vision, except as a minority in the workplace.

And, how the women of corporate India are way ahead of the curve, with their aspirations flying high and their conviction for leadership roles growing strong, and the rest of India needs to resonate, partner, and keep up with the dreams and visions of these 500 million women of India.

'A civilization is judged by how it treats its minorities' – Mahatma Gandhi

PASSIONS OF THE MIND
From Wall Street in Manhattan to Dalal Street in Mumbai: The Fallacy of Unconscious Bias

2

Passions of the Mind is the story of an extraordinary man – brilliant psychiatrist Sigmund Freud in the 1880's – who proved that some of the most exciting challenges aren't met on the battlefield or on mountain peaks, but inside the hearts and minds of individuals. Freud was one of Vienna's most distinguished neurologists who gave up a life of respectable affluence to become a daring researcher of uncharted seas – in an effort to change forever our understanding of human motivations, and free people everywhere from the blindfolds and chains of their unknown natures. He was a pioneer explorer of the dark frontiers of the sexual nature of humans, for which he was made a pariah.

There is no such thing as "unconscious bias" – all bias should be seen as "conscious" – as it leads to a "conscious action". All conscious discrimination needs to be penalised in a civil society – and not waived off as the result of "unconscious bias". Accountability for actions will be key to resolving them – no matter what is the genesis of the action – conscious or unconscious.

By targeting unconscious bias – societies are simply disregarding the need to take action against "conscious discrimination" being made against gender minority communities in the workplace.

*Is it a matter of "perception" that women do not opt for leadership positions in the choices they make – or is it the sign of a **conscious institutional bias** working against women in the workplace, that shows such unacceptably low levels of women in decision-making positions across academia, public offices, corporate boardrooms, and parliamentary democracies?*

Year 2010: New Delhi

There can be no better measure of the serious intent of companies to invest in the advancement of their executives and workforce – than the amount of budget that the company is allocating to training, mentoring, and leadership programs each year. In year 2010, we launched the *WILL-KPMG survey on "Women and Wealth Creation"* which reported that companies in corporate India – including multinationals operating here – were spending less than 5% of employee development funds on women executives, out of the total organisation investment that is budgeted by the human resources department. The rest of the funds were being spent on training programs for male employees. While endless arguments could be put forward about women leaving the workforce or leaking leadership pipeline, it does not change the depressingly low amount being spent on training, skilling, mentoring women employees across all levels of the organisation.

Further, this meagre investment is focused mainly on the "softer areas" of women development – as short-term operational interventions to improve the eco-systems for women – and less on the strategic long-term investment of building women's intellectual skills and abilities, as well as tangibles to enhance their overall working experience, which have far-reaching quantifiable benefits for the organisation. There is also no serious attempt by companies to measure the investment they are making in women – so no real-time data that can be valuably used to make an assessment is currently available. It is also reported that the companies were of the view that not enough women were registering to attend the leadership training programs, especially if the programs were residential and post-office hours.

Taking a Leaf out of The Wharton School Story:

Year 2011. Pennsylvania, USA

I received a distinguished scholarship to the prestigious six weeks Advanced Management Program at Wharton School, awarded in recognition of all the vision and work that we were accomplishing for the advancement of women in India. This was indeed one of the finest moments of my life – particularly for someone who has been educated with the elite and rigorous Delhi School of Economics professors, which while being truly world-class by all standards of econometric models and policy analysis – may have lacked the exposure to the "real-time billion dollars business world" that churns out "hot money" into billion-dollar companies, which in turn influences the direction of global economies from China, to Mexico, to Kazakhstan!

It was a great privilege to arrive at the "hallowed-academic hallways" of Wharton School, Locust Walk, at the University of Pennsylvania, on a distinguished scholarship award in year 2011 – which has a reputation for being founded in 1881 as the 'first collegiate business school, recognised globally for intellectual leadership and ongoing innovation across every major discipline of business education.' With broad global community participation and one of the most published business school faculties, Wharton carries the distinction of creating "economic and social value" around the world with a powerful alumni network of over 1,00,000 graduates and more than 9,000 annual participants in the Executive Education Program – to which I had received the scholarship

On the very first day – when we were introduced to the *Wharton AMP: Class of 2011*, it was interesting to find that there were about fifty top male executive participants from leading Fortune 500 companies registered for the program, and only a minority of four women participants in the group – almost all of whom were owners of their consulting companies except for one woman participant. Even for someone with my broad-bandwidth of exposure – with Visiting Fellowships at the Salzburg Seminar in Austria, SAIS Johns Hopkins University in Washington DC, and extensive travels across business communities and conferences in USA, Europe, and South Asia, that are largely male-dominated – I must admit that I was at a total loss on how to become accepted by this "heavily male dominated" class – where the four women participants were clear "outsiders". As the first-days of the Wharton AMP Program progressed – the male bonding groups, male-banter across classroom benches, beer-drinking evening networking among the male participants, fitness centres being full of male "workout" enthusiasts – it became apparent that the women participants had to literally find their way into breaking the male networks, or find patronizing men who would sponsor them into the buddy-networks – which was the last thing one expected in the elite hallways of Wharton school Executive Education, where the focus is on excellence in innovative academia for which the inclusive ideas of each participant should be worth their weight in gold! Even within the small break-out AMP Group to which the participants were allocated – the gender discrimination among women was visibly apparent– almost as if the ideas of the "minority view" were being tolerated – and visible articulation of ideas by women hardly encouraged.

I must also admit that I did not sense any conscious effort on the part of the distinguished facilitators at the Wharton AMP Program to try to help the women align with the group, in a seamless and embracing way – which would be the hallmark of any world-class Faculty who want to get the best from the "collective" energies of the group.

Speaking about the AMP Program Faculty – in the entire six weeks curriculum, there were only 1–2 women Professors on the distinguished Faculty that I can recall, and only 1–2 recommended background reading by women academics for the course materials. The lack of gender-diversity in the program, was further substantiated by the classroom teaching style – that was largely driven by male-dominated leadership stories of Napoleon, baseball, soccer, kayaking, and similar case-studies of male CEOs who found their "North Star" to success in business. Large billion dollar companies seemed to be investing mainly in their high-potential male executives for advancing their leadership skills over the year – as a "**conscious bias**", and MBA programs were therefore clearly being tailored to address the male mindsets as "**institutional bias**". Presently, nothing seems to have changed fundamentally in the allocation of these funds for tenured professors in the best management institutions worldwide, **which** continues to remain a mystery, when 50% of the **graduates** passing out of the best management schools today are women.

Recognizing Institutional Bias

One of the most vocal and accomplished women professors – on issues relating to public policy and civil rights – is my dear friend and colleague, renowned public administration scholar and author Professor Beryl Radin – McCourt School of Public Policy at Georgetown University, in Washington. I met Beryl Radin when she was a Fulbright Scholar to India in 1990, and was based at the Indian Institute of Public Administration in

Delhi, studying the structure and functions of the elite Indian Administrative Services as an instrument of federalism. Beryl Radin was one of the USIS Speakers that I was accompanying to several institutions, universities, and forums – as part of my job as Chief Program Officer at United States Information Service New Delhi. Much of my early years of understanding the roles and power of the civil rights movement in the USA, the institutional bias and discrimination faced by minorities in civil society, and the critical need for affirmative action – was influenced heavily by the very scholarly and yet emotionally –charged discussions with Beryl Radin during our long visits to the IAS Academy in Mussorrie, Allahabad and Kanpur universities, in India

According to Professor Beryl Radin, McCourt School of Public Policy, Georgetown University

'Institutional bias can be found in government agencies, private business corporations and universities as well as other institutions in a society. It can occur in formal policies as well as in informal behaviours.'

'Institutional sexism shares many attributes with institutional racism. It is found in the assumptions that those with power make about the role and presence of women in the organisation or function. It can be found in policies about hiring and promoting women in organisations. It is expressed in views about the appropriate behaviour of women as managers. And it clearly is articulated in the availability of facilities (such as women's rooms) for women.'

'Like institutional racism, these behaviours are embedded in the formal and informal practices of the setting. They rarely result from the behaviour of an individual and thus require a different strategy.'

The validation of a strong sexist bias in institutions was further confirmed when I met the passionate and highly accomplished Professor Dianne Bevelander, Executive Director of the EU

Erasmus Centre for Women and Organisation, at the Rotterdam School of Management –in September 2014 in the Netherlands. Diane's whirlwind energy, and complete understanding of the elements that continue to distract women from leading in business and academia in Europe and worldwide – found voice in the forums Professor Diane Bevelander conducts for women professionals across the Netherlands, stellar research, and the inspiration she continues to give to every woman she meets – including myself. Leading through innovation, Dianne has designed a Women's only elective at Rotterdam School of Management focusing on the empowerment of women aspiring to leadership roles using the mountain (Mt Kilimanjaro) as an outside classroom, and as a metaphor for business.

Professor Diane Bevelander has written extensively about her research that '**Business Schools are still very male dominated.**' She recently said in an interview:

'Most of the professors are male, most of the cases we use in class have one or more male protagonists, most of the textbooks and articles used are written by men. There are very few female role models.

At RSM, the President of the University and I are the only operational female role models and there are only three female Professors at RSM. As a consequence of this, it is perhaps not surprising that the initially nominated candidates for the honorary doctorates were all male. I started to ask, *don't you have any female candidates?* Last year I really pushed it. And I must add, some of the faculty were really supportive and helped a lot. So last year, for the first time, we gave an honorary doctorate to a female scholar!' The picture in academia remains depressing low even in the European Union, with only 13% of full professors in the Netherlands being women, putting a country renowned for its progressive attitudes ahead of only three other EU member states –

Belgium, Cyprus and Luxemburg – according to *She Figures 2012*, an ongoing European Commission report.

This also reminds me of the excellent experience shared by a senior most woman executive of the $4 billion Avantha Business Group in India, which operates in twenty-five countries in areas ranging from power transmission to paper production. As someone who is always invited to the top leadership company off-site meetings – she was reflecting that the "recreation time" for the Executive Management Team was always spent on playing a "good game of cricket". Since there were only two senior women in the leadership team of Avantha Group and since both of them did not play cricket – it was never thought that perhaps a more inclusive "women friendly" game can sometimes be included in the program recreation time. Perhaps a good game of chess? Badminton? Billiards? – all of which would pass as gender-neutral. Cricket has historically only been played by male sportsman – at the professional and commercial level – where cricket test-series and IPL cricket mania has become a large money –churning industry with male "honchos" betting on players on-and-off the field, and women watching as part of the "passionate cheering crowd".

It would seem naïve to pass-off these continuing practices in the workplace, management schools, and in business conferences – as "unconscious" bias – as it leaves no accountability for those who design, create, and implement these programs –under the banner of "leadership".

Year 2009: Pune

The only way out of this syndrome of low investment levels for advanced training of women – was for us to launch a distinguished world-class pioneering mentoring program for women in leadership in corporate India – that would be residential, cross-industry, and with a high registration fee and remarkable faculty of business leaders, so that companies have the opportunity and program to invest in their women. However, the very first time that I mentioned the women's leadership program proposal to the highly-credited HR Directors in corporate India, *they closed the conversation even before it had started.*

It became apparent from the very beginning – that all the buy-in for launching this program would have to come from the enlightened CEOs – who had a good understanding of the sustainability of their organisations, and the power of women to contribute to the company's progress. We then approached the stalwarts of corporate India – in the year 2009 – Mr S. Ramadorai, Chairman of Tata Consultancy Services, Richard Rekhy, CEO KPMG, and Board Directors of the Tata Group Dr J.J. Irani, who had a real understanding of good corporate governance and stakeholders interest – and took up the challenges of launching for the very first time in corporate India, a pioneering cross-industry residential program for fast-track women executives – and compelling the companies to invest in their women.

We launched the *5-Day Residential Cross-industry "WILL Creating Women Business Leaders" program* at the beautiful Tata Management Training Centre campus in year 2010 –that has now produced more than 650 WILL mentees from across leading Indian companies and multinationals, including Tata Consultancy Services, KPMG, Castrol, Sodexo, Robert Bosch, Microsoft, Genpact, GE India, Capgemini, Axis Bank, Merck India, Aditya Birla Group, Eaton Technologies, BNY Mellon, Starwood Resorts, Tata Steel, Amazon, and others.

Welcome to the Tata Management Training Centre, Pune

This enlightened academic think-tank and training institute of the powerful Tata Group was destined to became the first venue for the annual residential cross-industry WILL Creating Women Business Leaders programs when it was launched in 2009 – and has consecutively been a committed partner with the WILL Forum for the past six years – to bring together high-potential women and coalesce their energy, bonding, learning, distinction – like corporate India has never seen before!

Founded in 1959 by JRD Tata, the Tata Management Training Centre (TMTC) was set up with the mission for creating an executive class of leaders that would lead the large Tata Group companies with a common vision for excellence and sustainability. The Centre has a stunning colonial-style heritage structure, built on fifteen acres of sprawling green grounds in the city of Pune, that promises to "bring fresh air and fresh thinking" to all minds that care to take a walk among the serene surroundings of "green trees, green grass, and green leaves". With state of the art conference rooms, a traditional world-class library, colonial-style pillars, hand-crafted furniture, and the sounds of birds chirping in the wild greenery – TMTC is the ultimate residential campus for learning in excellence. What stands out most of the all at TMTC is the heritage of core values of integrity, understanding, excellence, responsibility – laid out by the Founding Fathers, that is carried with pride among the loyal and long-serving staff – from the gatekeeper to the TMTC Centre Director.

The executives and staff on the TMTC campus were clearly delighted to see so many smart women professionals from across different industries and sectors on their premises for the very first time in sixty years – where they had hosted only several groups of senior male managers and executive leaders from the Tata Group. The women brought a variety of "colours and diversity" to the environment and ambience, and seemed to be literally transforming the entire ethos of the TMTC campus, as they chatted, did the morning fitness yoga on the lawns, studied in groups on their homework through the night, and filled the TMTC elite Executive Dining Hall with the vibrant "bangles, saris, fragrance, stilettoes, and feminine fashions" that defined the differentiating style of women in leadership!

We would truly like to compliment the entire TMTC staff, who went out of their way to provide comfort, care, attention, excellent food, and good etiquette at all times for the fifty women participants. They also shared many stories of their wives and daughters at home – sometimes asking for guidance on what education to give their children, how their wives look after the house while they are at work, how they have devoted their entire lifetime of over fifty years to the Tata Group in the hope of raising their families and giving them a good life and progressive education. The one who stood out most was the seventy years old Mr. Khushru Tarapore, Dining Room Chief. His total dedication to looking after each and every guest in the Dining Room, asking about their "health and wellness" each morning, making sure that everyone got an explanation of the details of the menu, and simply saying "you look so fresh today!" – will make him an icon amongst the WILL Mentees who have passed the corridors and hallways of the TMTC campus, over the past six years.

But then, when it was time for the Tea Break on the first day of the five-day Residential Program – *where were the women's washrooms at the TMTC campus?* It became clear at our first mentoring program that even in year 2010, the Tata Group had not provided for an appropriate ladies washroom – just as there was one provided for the men, as they never imagined that there may one day be several women who are aspiring for leadership in corporate India! We had a few guest rooms opened for this purpose during the classroom sessions – and it surely left me wondering about the state of the minority of women executives who are working on the TMTC staff and faculty, as full-time or part-time employees. I am sure that they are visible, doing an outstanding job, and totally committed and dedicated to the Tata Group vision – but the equality of their aspirations was clearly not weighed in when the "men sat down to decide the power games of business". I must also mention that when we conducted the WILL Mentoring Program next year in 2011 – we saw a sparkling world-class, state-of-the art ladies' washroom on the TMTC campus.

This is why we call it "conscious bias". It is unconscious only as long as it remains within the limits of the mind – but when it is translated into "action" – it becomes a conscious bias with conscious consequence for the affected party and stakeholders. There is then no need to create window dressings, or blend it behind more verbal rhetoric – of "unconscious bias" which simply leads the dialogue to another track and places no accountability on those who have acted with conscious bias and discrimination in the community, organisation, or workplace.

Resolving the conscious bias in the workplace – will require fundamentally changing the eco-system in the workplace, and then validating the change by benchmarking the company against the best practices. These will be the "best employers for women" companies, who will not rely on the anecdotes and stories of HR leaders on how "awareness has increased in the workplace with respect to the roles of women". These companies will conduct a gender-leadership survey on the "gender-sensitivity" and cultures of their companies, and then put the "Fifty Best Practices for Women in the Workplace" that will be the fundamental hygiene for equal opportunity, advancement and promotion policies, and zero-tolerance for gender bias.

Year 2012: Bangalore

Meet Linsey Simpson, Head of Operations of Thomson Reuters in Bangalore, who I was visiting at her office, while trying to learn from someone who had demonstrated immense courage, conviction, and accomplishment that we all seek in the best business women in the corporate world. Linsey is one of the finest business leaders, and fully committed to advancing women in her Bangalore offices – and has been driving the agenda for inclusivity and diversity with great purpose at Thomson Reuters, including leading the internal women's networks personally and being an Oxfam Trailwalker fundraiser for women. It was then that Linsey mentioned that in spite of all the work that companies do to enhance diversity and women – there does not seem to be any measurable way to understand the progress on this, including the change in culture and mindsets if any – in order to plan for the road ahead.

This was an important seeding in our minds –where we understood how we need to **validate, verify, and measure** – the stated action the companies were **consciously** taking, and how much change has actually taken place after implementing the appropriate policies on the advancement of women. We wrote the report on *"Benchmarking Best Employers for Women" in 2012* – with partnership and sponsorship from GE India – and this set an important footprint for *escalating the dialogue on how companies and organisations can **verify and validate how much conscious action has been taken on their stated policies.***

The Question we set out to ask CEOs in India and worldwide is:

If everything is right – then what is wrong?

If all the policies and frameworks for diversity and advancement of women are in place – then why are the "numbers and metrics" not showing any increase?

It has taken several years – to try to transform the thinking of the senior leadership in companies that Meritocracy can be implemented – only after the validation of equal opportunity. Otherwise meritocracy simply promotes people selectively – and recycles the same candidates – in a conscious bias of selective-discrimination based on the subjective perception of the command-and-control leader. That is why corporate Executive Committee and Boardrooms – look exactly the same, homogenous, everywhere!

I have spoken to over 6,000 women professionals across the heartland of India in the cities of Lucknow, Jaipur, Coimbatore – and in the metros of Mumbai, Chennai, and Bangalore – and aside from a handful of women – there is a near consensus that "there is a lack of equal opportunity in the workplace" and so meritocracy has little relevance for the minority of women in the companies. What seems to be more painful – is the increasing trend towards marking outspoken women in the executive workplace as "activist" "feminist" or "radical" – and to try to keep them from being appointed to high level positions in the company, as they are perceived as "risky" and may "rock the boat".

Meet Sangeeta Singh, Independent Director on corporate Boards in India

One of the most articulate and real-time women who truly understands the status of women in corporate India –with over thirty-three years of experience in HR leadership, including KPMG, PwC, and others. Sangeeta is now serving as an

Independent Director on corporate Boards. She came to the first meeting of the "Forum for Women in Leadership" at the Infosys Technologies campus in Bangalore – and has been an actively campaigning for equal opportunity, and women's advancement, and the conscious bias in the corporate workplace, as a WILL Advisory Board Member.

According to Sangeeta Singh: 'The age old and much abused argument that men and women are equal but "it's just a division of labour" needs to be first killed before we can even try to accept that men and women are indeed equal. This ridiculous definition has allowed men to appropriate titles like "bread earner" and "housewife" making one respectful and the other derogatory. In our strife to gain equality we need to address the language used by everyone around and most of all by us.

Women aspirants deal with this blatant casteism in language at every stage – *are you married, when do you plan to start a family, who will take care of the kids, can you travel, can you work late, the project is in a remote location, etc.* Corporate India needs to change this language.

Corporate India needs talent, diverse skills, different temperament's, differing risk taking abilities, varied levels of aggression and an inclusive approach. CEO's accept that while all these are needed they are not all "male skills sets". Amazingly while they want the women to bring in these skills they want to be able to use them only up to the point they decide. Therefore, women are useful as members of the team but leaders are inevitably men!

The time to debate whether the glass ceiling exists or not is long gone. It is time to focus on the cure – let's find the solution. Talking about affirmative action or meritocracy is only going to hurt women aspirants. Corporate India needs to have separate programs to nurture and promote women leaders. They need to have timelines and targets for themselves and not aimless mentoring programmes. The proof can only be in data – real numbers of how many women leaders are there in each organisation and what percentage of top management they constitute.

Women leaders are nudging their male colleagues on this path of understanding. But it continues to be a steep uphill path. The support and inclusion needs to be accelerated in Corporate India.'

Taking a Leaf out of Europe: Austria, Slovenia, and Netherlands

Even smart European women professionals from Austria, to Slovenia to the Netherlands – seem to be averse to taking the risk of being viewed and branded by their colleagues as "articulate and visible" in the workplace – almost as if it were a threat-perception of the smart women rather a compliment to the women's productivity and talents. In a most excellent Women's Tea Meeting *in Linz, Austria, in 2012* – organised by the thoughtful academic Professor Gerhard Wuhrer, who was at that time Dean of the Management Faculty at University at Linz – I met a range of very talented, enterprising, and hardworking Austrian women professionals, in a lovely "cellar-style" restaurant – with perfect candle-light ambience, finest crystal from Vienna, and exquisite chocolates of Linz! During my presentation on how women should build their executive presence, get visible and articulate in the workplace to advance their careers – I was surprised to find at least half the group engaging with me in an intense discussion on how they might be putting their "careers at risk" if they positioned themselves as a "threat" to their male counterparts and peers in the company. It would seem that the women who were often the only earning mothers for their children – and the only "source of income for the food on the table" – were simply not willing to take the risk of "annoying" their male decision-makers in Europe, which is fully understandable. ***This is a conscious bias of gender-discrimination in the workplace.*** It is also a sad statement of the well-being and culture – for well-developed continents that seem to be way ahead of emerging economies like India, China, and Mexico –with established manufacturing and banking industries that produce world-class automobiles, airplanes, railways, and have some of the most profitable banking and financial systems. Could the women of Europe never have contributed to this business success of the EU – and why then is there wide spread gender-discrimination in Europe – that Norway and Scandinavian countries were compelled to pass a 40% quota-bill for women on boards?

In 2014: Lasko Spa, Slovenia

I visited the breath-taking Lasko, Spa Resort in eastern Slovenia, at the invitation of Dr Patricija Jancovick, a remarkable women who was totally consumed with transforming the way "municipalities" were performing in Slovenia and working hard to bring some sense into "sustainability" in breath-taking Slovenia. The enchanting Lasko town is located at the foothills of the Savinja River, and dates far back to 1227 – best known for its flowers, and vineyards, spas, and pure natural mineral waters.

Chairing the meeting was Mrs Katarina Kresal, a lawyer and founder CEO of European Mediation Centre, and a former member of Slovenian Parliament and Minister for Internal Affairs of the centre-left government of Slovenia. She has been proclaimed the "Slovenian Woman of the Year for 2009" by *Jana*, the oldest Slovenian women's magazine. Later, she stepped down as a Minister of Interior due to a political controversy, and did not enter politics again into the National Assembly. Ms Kresal's

presentation at the Women's Group meeting was both startling –
and disturbing. It was "startling" due to the candour with which
Ms Kresal spoke of her political career, how difficult it was her
to make her way "as a women" into the halls of male-dominated
governments, and how hard she had to work to make a "space
for herself". It was "disturbing" as she had clearly experienced
tough power-play among her male counterparts and the sad
"victimisation of women" that women in power experience, as a
minority in Parliament, across the world including Europe, that
brought down her political career.

*With all these endless perceptions, gathered from across
women and industry around the world – it became compelling
to find out how exactly we can deal with this "institutional
and conscious" bias – against women in the workplace, so that
successor generations of women be allowed to realise their full
potential, and opportunities – and societies and communities,
and families and businesses will thrive and progress!*

Year 2012: Perception vs. Reality

Benchmarking the "Conscious Bias" validation process

With this determined objective in mind, the WILL Forum began
a ground-level Survey to understand what are the "gaps" in the
stated policies with regard to women in the workplace vis-à-vis
their actual implementation and impact:

Finding 1:
*Patronizing Attitudes towards women: Majority of companies in
India and multinationals – are focusing solely on the "softer"
work-life issues for women in their HR policies, relating to:*
• Enabler Policies –Building the Eco-System for Women:

- Networking Internal Women's Groups
- Work Life Balance
- Policies relating to Maternity Roles for Women
- Safety for Women
- Employee Welfare

Companies are most comfortable doing only the soft aspects, mid-level career development, attrition figures, and happiness quotient for women – as if this was just one-more-task that the HR function had to perform, to stay on par with their peer groups.

Companies were clearly not looking at the "business case" for women – and shying-away from the core best practices for "advancing" and promoting women in the organisation decision-making process.

Finding 2:
Companies are not focusing on the essential policies that will "Advance Women in Careers" or for top-leadership positions. Only a minimum number of companies in the survey have shown HR processes for building ecosystem for women career advancements, through implementation of:

- Equal Opportunity in the workplace
- Gender leadership Assessment and gender-neutral assessment
- Corporate Disclosures for all employees on diversity metrics
- Advancing women in top management and in decision-making positions
- Gender Diversity on Corporate Boards
- Mentoring women for Leadership – rather than for soft areas like work-life balance

Finding 3:
There are huge differences between the "Stated Policy" by corporate HR and the "Perceived Policies" by the women –

*especially with respect to: Equal Opportunity, Level Playing
Field, Leadership and Gender-Neutral Performance assessment.*

Thus while companies claim to have all the best practice
policies for women in place – women believe that the policies
are not implemented "in spirit" and often not communicated
appropriately. These apply mainly to equal opportunity, meritocracy
in promotions, respect for women who return to the workplace after
maternity, opportunities for advanced management training, and
given "high responsibility-high risk jobs" on the front-line.

Finding 4:
*In most companies in India and multinationals there are no
"stated policies" on the critical issues of corporate disclosures
for women, gender leadership assessment, and gender audits.
The following key elements of validating an equal opportunity
workplace, are missing in most companies even today;*
- Corporate disclosures on women in leadership positions
- Opportunities for driving P&L Revenue and business operations
  for women
- Equal Opportunity for women in promotions to front-line
  positions
- Gender leadership Assessment across all functions of management
- Routine Gender audits by Chief Diversity Officer of HR
- Robust gender-sensitivity programs for male managers in the
  workplace

The 2012 WILL Survey was most revealing – to substantiate the
"gaps" in "perception" – among what the women considered to be
a level playing field with no gender discrimination – and what HR
leaders seem to think was a level playing field – where meritocracy
was the final word on promotions, rewards, and financial bonuses.

For the record, the **highest number of "negatives"** came for
the following questions to the Indian and multinational companies

operating in India – relating to best practices for women in the workplace:

➤ Does your Company have a "stated Policy" of Conscious Recruitment of women for open positions at all levels?

➤ Does your company conduct Routine Gender Audits by the chief Diversity Officer?

➤ Does your Company provide clear career-graphs for "fast-track" women to reach CEO, President, Senior VP, and Board positions – to ensure that they stay with the company and get the best performance from them?

➤ Does your company have "at least one women on the Interview Panel" for all posts, at all levels in the organisation?

➤ Does your company provide "Employee Rewards" and Recruitment Rewards Scheme, for more women to be launched in the organisation?

➤ Is it mandatory for first time managers to undergo any gender awareness/sensitisation training programs?

➤ Has the effectiveness of this program been measured?

➤ Are all company projects evaluated/ audited from gender perspective?

➤ Are metrics around gender mainstreaming a routine part of the organisations score card?

➤ Does your company release Number of Women on the Company Board, and target plan of women as Board Directors?

➤ Does your company release data on any targeted leadership development programs specific to women and percentage of women covered?

It was time to launch the pioneering and landmark *"WILL Best Employers for Women: Benchmarking" practice* – and provide corporates in India and worldwide the tool-kit for measuring their own effectiveness in bringing diversity and inclusive growth as a key business priority.

IN PURSUIT OF BALANCED LEADERSHIP
Womenomics: The Compelling Case for Women and Wealth-Creation

3

'As women secure more and more powerful posts in the marketplace,
   corporate culture will change for the better,
   becoming more collaborative and less competitive,
   more inclusive and less elitist,
   and more flexible in the way the work environment is run.
   The workplace will become more productive in the bargain.'

Women are the least use resource in the world – and that is just plain bad economics.

   It is not about the elementary "Talent pool" of women – it's about the high productivity, value, contribution, innovation, strategic thinking, and thought-leadership that women bring to business and society – that needs our urgent attention

Year 2012

Even after conducting more than 300 Roundtable meetings of the "Forum for Women in Leadership" with over 6,000 women and men participants, from more than 250 companies, and releasing 15 WILL Research Reports – CEOs and corporate India seemed to be fully satisfied with the anecdotal evidence they had on the "business case for women" – and most of them were simply relying on "cut and paste" presentations from the big-four consultants to focus on women as "talent" and women as "customers".

The business case for women – and men – however goes far beyond the realm of this simplistic talk churned out in exactly the same clichés and speeches by those who do not understand the most important element that we all know is called "productivity" – that defines the input-output model of good economics that also forms the basis of competitive business. The question that we were always asked by the "naïve fellowmen occupying the portals of decision-making in billion dollar companies" – was:

Can you show us the correlation between women and profits?
Question:

(a) Why is this question never asked for men in business?

(b) Why does business not understand that women are just like any other valuable "resource" that companies use in the optimization of their business and communities' welfare – and a return on investment was always possible to make, provided someone was willing to put in the intellectual capital and commitment to do so.

Women and Wealth-Creation: Time for validation

It is truly time for corporate India – and leading business corporations worldwide – to move from anecdotal evidence about the value that women bring to business, and instead providing compelling and rigorous economic measurement and the validation of this substantive value. This can be accomplished when real-time economists and macro-empirical business strategists review the way in which companies have been viewing the business performance dashboard over the past century – and look past the top-line figures of finance, revenue, employees, customers, investors and shareholders – to assess each segment that contributes to business profits and wealth-creation in terms of usable statistical functions.

This pioneering analysis of the "value of women to business" will show – without doubt – the critical and premium addition that each corporate resource, including women in the organisation, is contributing to the wealth-creation of the corporation. Companies that want to sustain their future competitive edge and leadership should be prepared to place a high degree of weightage on women as a key resource component of business strategy – and the economic value of women will be seen as "equal or no less" when compared to the other resources that corporate entities find critical to their survival today – including capital, talent, finance, technology and customers.

It is this lack of an "economic-function" for estimating the value that women bring to the organisation that has led to the continued "blind spot" of having women over-represented at the bottom of the corporation and under-represented at the top – in companies across the world and in India, the US, Europe, Australia, and the Asia Pacific. Women also continue to be the least-used resources within any organisation, company, country and the planet as a whole.

This was our task in 2012 – to provide the corporate world urgently with a "tool" to assess the returns on investment in women – one that can be placed in the hands of the CEOs, board directors, diversity officers, HR leaders, and all other segments of business – so that we can move the discussion forward from simple anecdotes and data to validation for investing in women on boards, senior leadership and decision-making positions.

And, we actually believed that equal opportunity, inclusivity and diversity leads to improved business performance and is socially the right thing to do for a civilised society.

The key challenge for Good Economists: Making the Irresistible Business Case for Diversity and Women

The most important challenge while making our presentations for the business case on the "value of women" to organisations – was really how to format this dialogue out of the standard simplistic "HR-speak" of "war for talents" – into the critical domain of Adam Smith's optimizing the resources for wealth creation and the classical economist David Ricardo's comparative advantage – for progressive, libertarian, market-driven emerging economies like India, as a critical business model for competitive growth.

Over three years of patience and perseverance, and over *100 WILL Forum Roundtable meetings* of continuous discussions on the same subject – attended by over 1,000 senior executives from over 250 companies –hosted by GE India, Tata Consultancy Services, Axis Bank, Microsoft, Starwood Resorts, MSD Pharma, Capgemini, KPMG, BlackRock, Thomson Reuters, Deutsche Bank Global Services, Deloitte, Monsanto – across Bangalore, Hyderabad, Chennai, New Delhi, Gurgaon, Coimbatore, Mumbai, Kolkata, New York, Paris – we began to urge senior leadership to change their language on women and diversity:

Balanced Leadership: Changing the language on women in the workplace

- From "noble cause" – to a compelling Business case of women as customers, suppliers, employees, investors, and producers
- From patronizing and supporting women – to advancing women in their careers
- From focus on Women and Leaking Talent Pipeline – to understanding the Economic Value of Women – and Women and Wealth Creation

- From Retaining and mentoring Women – to Promoting Women into decision-making positions
- From women as customers, markets, and consumers only – to Balanced Leadership and Equal Opportunity Eco-Systems, for inclusive growth
- From Women as "Talent" – to Women and Enterprise Risk-Management – To Balanced Boards for Good Governance
- From Mentoring Women in aspiration deficit – to mentoring male managers in gender-sensitivity
- It's a Governance Issue – not an HR Issue
- It's a CEO and Board Responsibility – Not a Diversity Responsibility

Then, we had to make a simplistic "Defining the Value of Women at the Workplace" – and tried to recycle this among all the various seminars, conferences, and roundtables on women and diversity initiatives. We then bolstered this with "numbers" for corporate India – and following is what the chart looks like:

Defining the Value of Women in the Workplace

The Key Areas where the value of women should be measured – as part of the business revenue model:
- ➢ Women for "Balanced Leadership" – for innovation, intelligence, and best performance
- ➢ Women for Business Talent
- ➢ Women as customers, suppliers, investors, and employees
- ➢ Women for Enterprise Risk Management – lessons from the financial downturn of 2009, questioning the ethical values of boardrooms with male majority
- ➢ Women for Diversity of Leadership Style – public-spirited, collegial, consensus building, risk-averse, community-building – better for board-positions

➤ Women for Flexible Workplace flexible minds, flexible time, flexible spaces!

When the above segments of the Value of Women to the Organisation are placed in a measurable econometric format, following is what the econometric function will look like, that allows detailed calculation on the return on investment in women up to 5–6 level derivatives. Just like any other business resource, companies should be free to estimate the business value of women to the organisation – if they still need to make the business case for women, and the return on investment on women.

FIGURE 1:

Womenomics: Measuring the Value of Women

Women = f Σ
- Diverse talent pool, skills, experience
- New leadership styles
- Differential Cultural business formats
- Collective and collegial thinking
- Diverse customers, investors, employees, stakeholders, markets, suppliers
- Flexible minds, flexible workspaces
- Innovative Business Thinking
- Public Spiritedness
- Customer base and spending power
- Investor Funds/ Pension Funds
- Risk-Averse– Rational Boards

Source: WILL-KPMG Report on "Assessing the Returns on Investment in Women" – 2012

The same econometric function format can be applied to the important measurement of the value of good governance and diversity to corporate boards. It is not important what "number" or "weightage" the company places on the variable in the chart below, the important thing is for companies to know that they can do this – and should in fact calculate it on an annual basis to find out how much "Women and Diversity" are adding to their business value, as a key best practice and resource function.

Measuring the Value of Good Governance and Diversity on Corporate Boards

Inclusive Governance= f Σ

- Diverse talent pool, Skills, Experience on boards
- New leadership styles
- Differential Cultural business formats
- Collective and collegial thinking
- **Diverse customers, investors, employees, stakeholders, markets, suppliers representation**
- Flexible minds, flexible workspaces,
- Innovative Business Thinking
- Public Spiritedness
- Customer base and spending power
- Investor Funds/ Pension Funds
- Risk-Averse– Rational Boards

How do we put a co-relation on this diversity and good governance?

For many years we have kept recycling the above economic function – at over hundred roundtable meetings with women and men senior executives, and business leaders – in the hope that someday we might get the CEOs to focus on the critical economic and business case for women.

However, either this simple economic function was beyond their understanding – or they simply did not care to understand. We never saw this function quoted in any other presentation – and spoken in this compelling way. All that we heard was a recycling of the same arguments at every forum of business, HR, chambers of commerce, IT functions – that there is a business case for women – and it was always about "talent" of women or "markets and customers" who are women.

Never was the argument escalated to the critical innovative thinking, strategic insights, public spiritedness, risk-management, sustainability, or wealth-creation segment that women bring to the table.

As long as we do not escalate the dialogue on the value of women – and their innovative thinking and productivity – the discussions on advancing women will remain focused on patronizing attitudes towards women friendly policies, and the "right thing to do" – and will miss the entire compelling need for national development, progress, of which women are equal contributors – as much as the receivers of the benefits.

Year 2013

We decided to write the **WILL-KPMG Report on "Women and Wealth Creation"** – so that every CEO could have a written document that could help them *quantify* the "business value" – which is not the same as the "business case" – for women in leadership positions, and how to measure the return on investing in women.

The WILL Balanced Leadership Value Model, as an econometric function for quantifying the value of women to business, is shown in detail in Annexure 2, page 210.

THE GENDER-CONTEXT OF LEADERSHIP
Talent is Universal – Opportunity is not

4

'Talent is universal, but opportunity is not.
And in many places, opportunity is still out of reach for women,
No matter how smart they are, how hard they work, how much encouragement they
might be given even by their own families, that it is still a very difficult task.'

Hillary Clinton, … at the Female Heads of State and Foreign Ministers Luncheon, 24th September, 2009

'Remember the high responsibilities of your desires.
No one can give to you
What you do not have the capacity to take.'

– Sarojini Naidu, first Indian woman to become the President of the Indian National Congress and the first woman to become the governor of a state in India.

Bangles, saris, fragrance, stilettoes:
Embracing the differentiating Style of Women in Leadership!
Mothers, daughters, wives, sisters –
All roles can be played, at the same time – and with distinction

Women do not need mentoring because they are deficient
Women need mentoring because the eco-system is unequal
in the workplace

Marriage – sacrifice-dedication:
How does this equation work for advancing women in leadership?

Year 2008

I was always enamoured with a lovely lady at one of the Travel Desk of the recently built Bangalore airport, where I used to often hire a local car for my day's business meetings in the city. She was always meticulously dressed in a *Kanchipuram* silk saree, with jasmine in her hair properly tied-up, and most courteous and efficient in taking notes of the customer travel requirements – and handing me the *receipt* when my turn came, and passing the instructions to the taxi driver who was to accompany me. As I had now seen her several times that I travelled via Bangalore airport – one day I asked her how many hours she works, and what else she plans to do in life – as she is so good at her job. She looked at me – and suddenly tears swelled up in her eyes. She told me that she was a Bachelors in Engineering and always wanted to keep working in the science and engineering field – but had to give up her dreams as she has a small son, with no one to take care of him – as her husband was at work all day. I asked her why she did not get some house-maid to assist – and her answer was as expected: *her husband was the bread-earner in the family, and her place was in the home.* She works only part-time at the airport travel desk – till her son returns from school.

How many such women engineers there may be, who could not use their meticulous qualifications to build productive and innovative careers in business, academia, and communities – and who may be able to draw immense benefit from mentoring with support groups and networks of other professional women, and gain confidence, articulate their requirements, and learn how to cope with their careers.

At the Cummins Women's College of Engineering – which is tucked away at a busy neighbourhood in the city of Pune – I had the fortune of conducting a series of "Women in Leadership" workshops for the women engineering students. The women students were all exceptionally bright, very optimistic, and full of aspiration and energy – during the course of the group sessions. However, at the time of individual interactions – I was stunned when many of them asked me to guide them on how they would cope with their parent's demands for them to get married at an early age, when they passed out of the engineering college. I was even more mystified when they told me that the engineering degree was a way to enhance their "marriage-premium", and that is the only reason why some of their parents had agreed to let them do the engineering course!

It occurred to me then, that a little time spent on mentoring these young women engineers, and reformatting their aspirations and capabilities – will go such a long way in saving their careers and teaching them to speak up their motivations, have confidence in their life goals, and build career roadmaps for themselves.

The "Hungry Women of the IT industry"

And then there are the thousands of "hungry women" in the fast-growing IT-software industry across the entire Indian nation, who have been working for eight to fifteen years in back offices of large multi-million dollar software companies and servicing large million dollar client accounts worldwide. These senior women executives are sometime not even given an "official designation", but addressed as "Consultants" – although they are full time employees receiving good incomes and salaries. These women are hungry for visibility, recognition, front-line jobs, and risk-reward functions – but are being simply "swept under the carpet" – *in their own words*. They have no opportunity to "raise their hand" – as they have a small reporting line to business unit heads, which are four to five steps away from the CEO of the company. These women clearly do not stand a chance of ever moving up in their careers – if they do not receive any formal mentoring from external coaches or programs – who can teach them how to build their executive presence in the company – and have a robust career roadmap just like their male counterparts.

A good case in point is the fact that all the big four IT Indian companies never had a women on their Board of Directors – until the Indian Companies Act of 2013 mandated one women on the board, as a key compliance. Even then, most of them waited till the last month of the deadline –to complete this appointment of a woman board director. Clearly, they are not looking for advancing the women in their organisation – and the IT-industry companies quarterly media reports are full of all-male interviews, all-male platforms, all-male TV shows, and all-male visions for the Indian IT in the coming years.

The largest IT company in India Tata Consultancy Services has 100,000 women in the company, which is one-third or 33% of the total TCS workforce. However, they have only a low 11% women in the senior leadership – and this does not include the company board of directors. What shall we expect from the other excellent software women engineers in TCS – who are spread across the two-tier cities of Bhubaneshwar, Coimbatore, Chennai,

Jaipur? Similar is the case for the Indian IT major Wipro, which seemed satisfied for so many years without a having a woman on their board –and all their "diversity programs" being focused on wellness and work-life balance for women. Same is the case for owner-promoter HCL Technologies – which is presently showing a poor ratio of women in the organisation. The only company that seems to be doing exceptionally well is the IT-related Genpact – with over 28% women in senior leadership – and robust program for recruiting, advancing, and moving women to the corporate board positions.

Many women from the Indian IT-industry had long conversations with me, over the past seven years – and their questions remain the same:

- Their simple aspirations to just get promoted to higher levels after fifteen years of service
- Their quest is to someday have a chance to work with CEO-led and the senior leadership teams
- Their aspiration is to be appointed as independent board directors in other companies, if they cannot get to their own companies' boards
- Their need for opportunities to get visible in IT-forums and platforms – as "mainstream" speakers – rather than "diversity" speakers
- Their need for exposure to other women across industry – in multi-company forums
- Their need to simply get applauded from peers across industry – for the good work that they do – with dedication and value addition – beyond the "internal" website company listings – that nobody really reads outside the company
- Their need to make a powerful contribution to national progress, the country, the society, the community and the women around them.

This is why it is critical for women to have mentoring
    Not because they are not talented – or the women are
"deficient" or "dysfunctional" in some way
    But because the women work in an unequal eco-system, with
pressures from society and families, stereotypes in the workplace,
and male-dominated systems where women literally do not stand
a chance of being "seen or heard"

This is the "Gender-Context of Leadership" for women
    And it is clearly different context from the men
    The DNA of male and female leadership is the same
    But both need to "manifest" them in different ways – because
the "context" of the workplace, its power-networks, and strategic
functioning – is different for women and men.

Why are there so few women in leadership positions…?
    Because: Men in black suits – will give awards to men in
black suits!

My encounters with a cross-section of over 6,000 senior and
middle women executives from corporate India – over the course
of about 200 WILL Forum meetings – left me simply mystified
with the status quo of seeing so few women at the industry CEO
meetings, chambers of commerce, legislatures, public offices,
academic professors, board directors, institution directors. It was
always *"men in black suits – networking with men in black suits"*

It also left me wondering why I was often the "only woman in
the room" – during my twenty-five years of high-end career work,
as CEO of my company, Independent Board Director on other
companies, public policy leadership areas, Visiting Fellow on
conflict resolution dialogues, and particularly as Speaker in several
corporate business forums where women were simply sitting on
the last bench in the room – practically invisible.

Part of the answer came to me when several women I met at conferences where I was a Speaker, would approach and ask me almost with eager guidance on 'why are you so un-inhibited? How do you speak so openly and passionately in front of such important people?'

My quick response to them was always:
'Why are you not like this?
This is the natural state to be for everyone
I do not see any barriers – where they do not exist
I have conviction – because I have done my homework, got my accomplishment, and distinction –
So what is there to stop me?'

As the best-selling author Ayn Rand famously said:
'The question isn't who is going to let me
It's who is going to stop me...'

But then – Reality-Bytes are about listening to the hundreds of women professionals across companies, academia, government, civil society – their angst and their frustration – their conflicts about being aggressively visible at the cost of being seen as "threats" to male counterparts, and their humble submission into just going along with the flow rather than meet the "sting of rejection". This would have been almost depressing for anyone, if not seen from a positive point of view – on how we can move forward on redeeming the excellent women from this vicious circle.

From leading metros cities of Mumbai and Bangalore – to the second-tier cities of Coimbatore and Lucknow – the story of the women professionals remains the same in India. It was as if the women were resigned to never be part of the leadership story in their organisations, always saw men only as heads of corporate business functions and boards, and did not see anyone looking "like themselves" in the hallways of corporate power-broking. The women professionals in India are usually quiet, not articulate, not visible, and do not make any attempt to be exceptionally heard – lest they get targeted by the dominant male peers and counterparts. One would never know – by even spending an entire day with them – that they were qualified engineers, chartered accountants, HR specialist, successful entrepreneurs, scientists working in nuclear technology and medical research, and managing billion dollar client accounts for their companies.

Meet Professor Zeeshan Amir, Director, GBMS Management Institute, Lucknow

Zeeshan is one of the brightest women entrepreneurs from the small tribal town in the heartland of central India, which makes the world famous carpets and where carpet weaving is the core of their livelihood. I met Zeeshan Amir over tea at the India International Centre, when she had applied in year 2000 for the Eisenhower Fellowships in India, and I was interviewing her as the India Special Consultant at EEF. Zeeshan spoke about the number of women in the small and backward town of Mirzapur in the state of Uttar Pradesh – who were unemployed, and has no real training or skill to their advantage. Zeeshan has opened a Training Centre for these women – for making embroidery and cloth work – so that they can remain occupied and earn a small income for their families and children in an honourable way. This was a truly challenging and most honourable thing to do – but Zeeshan got little recognition from the academic community there and little encouragement from any medium scale business group, to support her work.

She subsequently left Mirzapur to take up a teaching job as Professor of Management and Dean, Faculty of Management

Studies at the Integral University, in Lucknow – a Muslim Minority institution in the state capital city of Lucknow, and saw this as a great opportunity to contribute to the advancement and progress of the minority communities and issues relating to women empowerment. However, she slowly realised 'all these designation were ornamental to correct their gender ratio on paper.... "My voice was constantly being ignored, criticised or dismissed during the male-dominated meetings." – she says.

Over the years, a number of lady intellectuals joined and left or were forced to leave through coercion. Zeeshan decided to resign and go back to Mirzapur, and place her attention and effort on advising and aiding her NGO to upgrade and scale up the organisation for women of the minority and underprivileged communities.

It would therefore not be judicious – and may even be dangerously ignorant – to continue to blame the smart and educated women for their low-level of evident self-esteem or aspiration deficit – as they need to face gender discrimination at all levels in the workplace up to the highest levels of decision making, and need strong nerves, and strong commitment, and strong energy to keep them going.

The question is – why should this be the case – and where will we start "resetting the national moral compass" – on respecting, rewarding, and recognising women?

The ET Awards for Corporate Excellence in India:
Fuelling the male-leadership Syndrome:
Year after year –the glittering Economic Times Awards for business excellence are held at the Oberoi Towers in Mumbai – where all the "stars" of Indian business and politicians are invited to "praise each other" for their contribution to national progress, sustainable growth, and business leadership – covered

by the media, television, and splashed across the daily national newspapers. And, year after year, the ET Awards are usually given in corporate India to all male awardees; by all –male juries, and all –male speakers aside from a few women business participants and CEO spouses sparklingly dressed for "cosmetic addition". In fact, the former Honourable Finance Minister of India P. Chidambaram said in his speech at the ET Awards in 2013:

'Before I address the audience, I must specially thank the five women in the first row, the two in the second row, the five in the third row and all the men who outnumber women. I come from a city which I think is more gender sensitive than Mumbai. It is important to recognise that this kind of bias is there in every field of activity in India, and unless we recognise this bias, not only against women but against many other sections of the people, it will be difficult to understand the complexity of governing India.'

Clearly no one at the ET Awards was listening to Mr P. Chidambaram, as nothing much has changed in 2015.

India is also perhaps still the only country where the business leaders are referred to by the media as "Business Honchos" – which denotes a person in charge of some group that is usually of male gender. The Prime Minister still invites the "captains" of Indian business, for all India Business Roundtables, which are mostly all-male events. India's national Apex software association NASSCOM is still to see a women President, and same goes for several national Chambers of Commerce in India, including the twenty-eight years old national HRD Network. Among the top 500 companies listed on the Bombay Stock Exchange – there are less than 10% woman CEOs in India, many of whom are wives of owner promoters. The large number of women CEOs in the Indian banking industry is also misleading – as many of them are heading multinational banks like HSBC, Bank of America, JP Morgan.

It is time for us to create and celebrate large volumes of about 50,000 women business leaders and professionals in India– instead of celebrating the few role model women CEOs who make it to the Forbes most powerful women's list. The women CEO's have unfortunately made little impact on changing the dynamics of majority-male-based leadership, and have taken little initiative in mentoring the successor generation of women and inspiring them on the scale that is required, and sharing their knowledge vastly and with passion among the women's groups.

Teaching Penguins how to Fly!
Meet the women leaders who have passion – for improving the lives of other women:
Meet Rekha Seal, Chief Ethics Officer of Tata Steel, who has spent more than thirty years at Tata Steel, and has been a silent crusader of women's empowerment. I met Rekha Seal during the "Council on Corporate Governance" meeting in Mumbai, as was struck by her modest demeanour of starched cotton sarees, but a hot-fire within to bring ethical practices to corporate India – almost as a lone voice in a country where "bribery and corruption" have been the nexus between politics and businesses. Rekha told us about how she was mentoring women in the deep heartland of the city of Jamshedpur, where she was located at Tata Steel, the inertia that sets in with women who have spent more than two decades in the same position, with nowhere to go for career advancement – as all the top-brass of the company was all-male.

We visited the lovely Tata Steel campus in Jamshedpur, an icon of how business needs to look after its communities – where we launched one of our first internal *"WILL Executive Education for Women"* for the women professionals of the company. A four-hour train ride from Kolkata, Jamshedpur is practically a "Tata Steel city" – where the company has built infrastructure, housing, schools, public utilities for the community of people who work at Tata Steel – and is a shining example of companies embracing the communities of their employees as part of the larger purpose of "corporate social responsibility". The one-day mentoring program with about fifty women professionals at Tata Steel gave me – and other member of the WILL Mentoring Faculty from KPMG, Monsanto, and Deloitte – our first glimpse of just how much the women in large companies get "comfortable" in their existing jobs, balancing the home and workplace, and being completely content coming to work every day and keeping themselves "productively occupied". They are fed upon the genuine benefits of being "dedicated" to their work – and finding comfort in the distant rewards of making an important contribution to society, family and communities.

But our one-day mentoring – seemed to have awakened their aspirations once again – and by the end of the day – we were astounded by the vast number of stories from each one of the women on how they had forgotten their "courage", how they needed to find a "sharp purpose", how we had given them a "second-awakening", and some of them even got so emotional over their "loss of purpose" and ambition, and search for excellence.

This then gave us validation – of what we already knew.

The women executives in corporate India were like "worker bees" – dedicated to their work and almost oblivious of the important need to rise to their full potential, enhance their self-confidence and self-esteem, retrain themselves for higher positions, opt for front-line visible positions, and contribute to the company's full potential.

The whole work-life and "family-responsibilities" syndrome was just a cover – for keeping women from aspiring to the top jobs – as less than about 12% of corporate India's women executives are in the early-age entry into the careers and motherhood. Most of the women who are stuck in mid-level jobs are in their early forties, with grown up children, if only the company would give them an "opportunity" on a level playing field to demonstrate and display their talents.

We have now completed several such internal mentoring programs for women across companies in Robert Bosch, Tata Teleservices, Metlife, Genpact, Barclays, Tata Consultancy Services, Total Oil, Citigroup, and others. No matter what the level of women participating in the mentoring programs – the profile and aspirations are almost always the same. What is also remarkable – is how a small "push" in the right direction almost always changes the mindset of the women in just one-day – and how they blossom with their new-found confidence, roadmap, energy, executive presence, visibility, and commitment to "move their waters".

From Mumbai to Paris – What we have learnt after mentoring more than 1,000 women in the workplace

- It is not about having dialogues and events on women's empowerment
- It is not about inclusivity discussions
- It is not about teaching women about work-life balance and time-management
- Or Emotional Intelligence
- Or listening to their challenges at work and at home
- Or their situations at office or networks
- Or how to deal with gender-discrimination
- Or providing crèches in the workplace or maternity benefits

These are "hygiene factors" – which should be fundamental to the company and factored into the **code of conduct of the organisation** – that will lend high support to the women at all times.

- *Mentoring women is about showing women the "power of self" and how to "unleash" their potential without boundaries*
- It's like teaching "Penguins how to fly"! Women have wings – but like Penguins they think they are only their "arms"
  It's about showing women how to understand their internal values and "brand",-and visibly demonstrating and displaying it with distinction
- It's about teaching women the art of influence and strategic communication – that they never placed a premium on – being only focused on "performance"
- It's about teaching women that "humility" is fine – but it's important to take credit for what you do – and that is called accountability and integrity
- It's about getting women vast exposure – and building a vast bandwidth of interest where others can "plug and play" when required
- It's about building "stiletto networks" that will support women in time of need
- And most of all – it's about finding the "courage, commitment, and confidence" – that they once knew, which brought them to the workplace against all odds of our socio-cultural environment.

Celebrating Penguins Who Learnt to Fly

Meet Jayashree Satagopan, Chief Financial Officer at International Paper, a qualified Chartered Accountant, and WILL Mentee: Batch of 2010.

I met Jayashree Satagopan when she was a senior executive at the supply-chain at GE in Bangalore, and was also seconded to leading the GE Women's Network Hub for South India. She invited me to address the senior male GE executives in Bangalore –

and we were fully determined to show them the very elementary work that the GE Women's Hub was doing – and escalate the dialogue for advancing women in leadership. We could have been "talking to the walls" – as almost all the fifteen –odd men in the room were constantly watching their mobile phones, or drinking "soda" – and it was evident that they had little interest in partnering for the advancement of women, in any way. I am sure that much has changed in GE India on diversity best practices, since those days. Jayashree was also one of the WILL Mentees – who must be complimented for driving the agenda for diversity and inclusion in GE on her return from the WILL Mentoring program, and one of the few Mentees to come back to the program as a WILL Mentor!

On the important issue of Mentoring Women in the Workplace, Jayashree shares her Mentoring Experience:

'Women have a distinct need for coaching and mentoring. Corporate world is still male dominated, especially in senior leadership and board positions resulting in predominantly male oriented leadership styles and culture. Women in leadership, often in a minority position tend to adopt to male leadership styles losing their authenticity and fundamental balance sometimes experiencing doubts about the effectiveness of their own leadership styles. Women also receive or ask for less constructive feedback which will help them to improve their performance and grow. Women at times go through the "Perfectionist Paradigm Syndrome" which makes them feel inadequate. Given the socio-economic conditioning, lack of a proper eco system to support their career ambitions, prioritizing work and life is an area where aspiring young women leaders need some guidance. Creating the impact and visibility, feeling confident and reassured, addressing the subtle biases and leadership dilemmas – are few areas where most often women leaders need some mentoring."

Our personal experiences with mentees is that many of them required the following key components:

- a reassurance about their confidence, conviction and courage
- skills required to negotiate, navigate and nurture
- the ability to take control, collaborate and command
- being one's own self – balanced, brave and beautiful self

Mentoring has been most effective on personalizing the conversation, sharing examples, getting them outside the comfort zone, stressing the need of being current and relevant, reiterating the importance of building networks and relationships, putting career in the forefront, building a personal brand, not shying to ask and encouraging to look into new horizons and greater heights. Several of them continue to stay in touch and the mentor mentee relationship has become stronger and more meaningful.

Corporate culture is twice as important as individual mind sets to determine whether women believe that they can succeed. Conducive corporate environment is where gender biases are eliminated / minimal – be it unspoken or unwritten. Gender intelligence and sensitisation among senior leaders and male managers are an integral part of creating a congenial environment where everyone's contribution will be equally valued.

To be impactful, these programs have to be handled in a very inclusive way and focused on better overall performance for the company and not driven just as women's agenda. Gender intelligence sessions could focus on valuing gender differences professionally and personally, being aware of personal values that affects one's work and perception of gender at work, identifying associated stereotypes on gender roles and looking beyond to shatter such stereotypes, identifying own actions and reactions that create barriers in a productive work environment, and steps to eliminate such barriers.

Mentoring male managers has to be done in a highly

professional manner as most senior male managers tend to shy away from or ignore such conversations as they find it threatening to their philosophies and beliefs. It has to be a gradual, step by step process enabling them to see the value that balanced leadership can bring to table. This is best done and most impactful, when there is a commitment from the CEO to the cause.'

Meet Ranamala Palepu – VP, Global Practice and Solutions Leader, IT Managed Services, Genpact USA, and WILL Mentee: Batch of 2009

Ratnamala Palepu is one of the senior most women of Genpact, who is most recently based out of New York, servicing clients with million dollar accounts for her company. She came to the first WILL Mentoring Program at Infosys Leadership Institute in 2008, when she was a mid-level executive at Genpact. Having watched her progression over the years – it is clear that Ratnamala was fully determined to use all her energy and dedication, work hard at Genpact, and get a good assignment that she richly deserved.

Here is what Ratnamala has to say on her experience in corporate India:

'The value that women bring in to corporate senior leadership roles is acknowledged, and though slower than needed, is getting better year by year. Since many customers have women in leadership roles even the laggards in this matter are now ready to re-wire to the new reality. Emotional intelligence, the design think, the aesthetics, retail, healthcare, wellness industry, the buying decisions and many more good reasons are forcing companies to think holistically. There is a strong need for diverse groups to think of innovative solutions to new business challenges and provide products and services that exceed customer expectation in an ever changing world. We have enough proof of how important it is to *the profitability of an enterprise. It is key to find the right diverse talent and value the differences.*

What will be the features of best employers for women companies? – An Organisation that leverages the differences that a diverse group brings to the table to create economic value, gives a fair chance to grow and lead, includes in decision making, has a purpose that they belief in and are proud of being part of. All the women want in corporate India – is a fair chance to lead and take on meaningful roles in senior management and C level.

Women need mentoring because they are juggling multiple hats and priorities in an employee life cycle. They are wired a little different and need an environment that recognises the difference and leverages that. A mentor goes a long way in making that adjustment in various life situations and helps navigate the organisation opportunities based on merit and performance of course.

The only way to bring about change is a radical mindset change in both men and women – and it is good to notice this change. Technology is also playing a key role giving many more channels to network which were not there some years back

In moving so far up into the corporate ladder I largely worked in two organisations – in the twenty-five year journey of work and career, it was important for me and I was fortunate to be in organisations with strong values and purpose and pioneering. I had an opportunity to do multiple roles that kept me fully engaged and two things that mattered were growing successfully and making a difference.

My few must Do's while at work:

Clear Goals, execution is key, outcomes matter, focus on few things but do it really well.

Keep an open mind while interacting with people and value different points of view.

Empowerment and collaboration are two dimensions that helped me drive significant results.'

Learning from the vast range of experiences and insights from leading corporate women executives in India, we have the following **WILL Roster on** *"why do women need mentoring for leadership"*:

- Lack of level-playing field in organisations
- Gender – stereotypes in the workplace and gender-bias at top-management
- Male-dominated corporate networks
- Lack of support from senior management for diversity and inclusivity in the workplace
- Invisible glass-ceiling that leads to de-motivation among women
- Aspirational-deficit among women due to socio-economic conditioning
- "Sting of rejection" in the past
- Motherhood pressures and feeling of guilt for children
- Understand the women's advantage and differential leadership styles that can be leveraged
- Build skills to navigate the "labyrinth" and corporate dynamics
- Need to share how other women are responding to these pressure and learn from their experience
- There is strength in numbers– and high energy in bonding, where there is a gender minority

Our experiences with interacting and dialogues with women across industry through structured roundtables, Open Tea House Meetings, mentoring programs, women on corporate boards series, conferences and seminars – has made us acutely aware – that there is an urgent and compelling need in corporate India to create 50,000 women business leaders– instead of celebrating the few role models that will make no impact on changing the dynamics of majority-based leadership.

And it is not about "mentoring women" – it's about "mentoring women in leadership"

This is the critical distinction that corporate India has to make – when starting and conducting programs for mentoring women.

The context must be clear – we are speaking about the "Gender – context of Leadership" – not about "Gender"!

USER'S GUIDE TO MENTORING
Learnings from Celebrating 650 WILL Mentees women professionals ...across Corporate India

5

Mentors are those who can reshape your thinking,
Take your mind to a higher level,
Put some nurturing into your "soil" into which you will plant the tree of life,
Show you possibilities you did not see,
Release your boundaries and set your mind free,
Push the horizon of your sensibilities,
Show you how to imagine, ignite, inspire, indulge yourself.
Mentors are not teachers, coaches, preachers, guides, or role models –
Mentors are the oxygen of life – itself.

As a sharp, practical and rigorous economist – I have never had any interest in mentoring, and never had any mentors who could proxy for my capabilities. I have always thus led my life with high accountability and integrity – to take credit for what are our accomplishments, and take full discredit where we have failed to deliver to our stakeholders, families, communities, and fellow well-beings.

I was therefore mystified when I heard all around me in year 2007 – when we launched the WILL Forum – the incessant discussions at every meeting on how women need mentoring, need to have forums and platforms for networking and counselling, need to share their work-life issues, build confidence, self-esteem, executive presence, and simply learn to be visible.

Giving Cross-industry Exposure to Women:
The Critical Missing Link in Leadership

2009, Mysore

I met Aruna Newton, Chief Learning Officer, at the breath-taking, word-class Infosys Leadership Institute at Mysore – which is about two-hours car-drive from Bangalore airport. We got together to conduct the ***experiential first cross-industry residential*** pioneering program in India – with a group of fifteen women executives from Genpact, Citigroup, ONGC, Bank of America, Zensar Technologies, Infosys, Nokia, KPMG, Dr Reddy's Labs – with a high-level distinguished Faculty of serving CEOs and business leaders, over a period of five days.

Each day, each moment, each discussion, and each conflict – during the five days program – left an indelible mark on our minds on "redefining mentoring for women" – and we knew then that women are not being taught how to release their power, how to advance their interests, how to build their confidence, how to get distinction and exposure. Instead they were relegated to elementary discussions about work-life balance, and psychological "soft" issues – that would keep them satisfied in their current positions. Over candle-light bonding dinners at the green-trees of Infosys Mysore – and over long walks at midnight pondering over where we were going with this program – we were reinventing our own minds on why women need mentoring and therefore how a mentoring program for women should be structured. We also got enormous knowledge from the Master of the *Bihar School of Yoga and Fitness Master Sumit Kumar, Director of FMC India*– who led us into the unknown worlds of "work and work-out" during the morning yoga sessions of meditation and endurance. The "work and work out" sessions have now become an important part of all the residential mentoring programs for women – aligning the mind and body toward the "power of self".

Case Study: World Class Learning Experience for women professionals

Components of the WILL Mentoring Program: Creating a "Learning Experience"

The aim of any impactful and meaningful mentoring program for women executives – should be to provide the opportunity for strengthening and aligning the varied aspects critical to achieving success and advancement for women executives in their professional roles. In this highly interactive, personal, and experiential voyage, participants begin to gain a deep understanding of the leadership approach, negotiating style, cultivating responsible-power, and enhancing relationships and the network structure.

The Program builds an increased self-awareness in participants with a better sense of well-being and more effective leadership personalities. The "Creating Women Business Leaders" successfully enhanced the Awareness factor needed to recognise and transcend the barriers of limitation, so that goals can become realities. By examining leaders' challenges through a feminine perspective, women executives were better able to appreciate "when and why gender matters" in organisational and personal advancement.

The Mentoring Program Vision

❖ to build women business leaders who are accomplished, contributing, and with a global mind-set that will add value to the organisation and the society in which they work.

❖ to nurture and guide senior women executives from who are nominated by their companies, to engage with cross-industry peers and learn from each other's experiences and from the distinguished leadership faculty of our Knowledge Partners and the WILL Mentoring Council.

❖ to provide the opportunity for strengthening varied aspects critical to achieving success and advancement for women executives in their professional roles; and build an increased self-awareness in participants with a better sense of well-being and more effective leadership personalities.

Principles of an Effective Mentoring Program

❖ *Learning Leadership:*
  o *Leadership is best learnt through a focus on experience, role models, action oriented content and finding relevancy*
❖ *Adult Learning Model*
  o *Provide learning through all modes: didactic, experiential, conversation, group exchange, simulation, reflection (public and private). Faculty approach should balance between directive and facilitative*
❖ *Learning with Women*
  o *Capturing the experience of women, providing a common learning foundation, building across function and expertise, building across generations and learning from the experience of other women.*
  o *Incorporate all social contexts for learning, connect with self-regard and self-concept, allow learning to use personal voice in dialogue with others, consider women's connections to enhance learning,*
  o *Clear goals, operate with autonomy, respectful of all learning styles, building on experiences, self-directed, stretching and supportive*

Program Enablers for the participants

❖ *Explore and examine who they are as leaders in different contexts*

❖ *Increase "Individual Capital" by discovering their strengths*

❖ *Enhance "People Capital", by actively building and growing self and others, and creating vibrant relationships*

❖ *Learn to enjoy the leadership voyage, find their energy-source and discover-manifest happiness for themselves, using constructive frameworks*

❖ *Enhance their "Presence" and build confidence for risk-taking and embracing opportunities*

❖ *Appreciate the way in which gender impacts the exercise of authority in a group or organisation*

Best Practice PROGRAM THEMES

FIGURE 2:

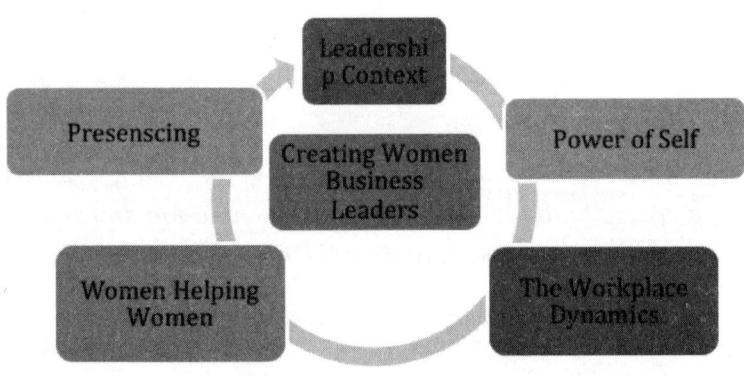

Theme 1: The Leadership Context

"It is said that the last thing that a fish is likely to discover is the water it is swimming in." The question here is: like the fish, do we take our context for granted?"

As women leaders who have a role to play in shaping and setting the organisational context, it is imperative that we explore and understand the milieu and environment in which we have evolved our leadership.

Developing the ability to read and decipher the forces that have shaped our lives as women and leaders will result in women becoming more aware of the contexts that need to be created NOW. Exploring the question of 'what type of context is being created by your leadership?', will lead to building "contextual intelligence" – the ability to understand the influence of the contextual forces surrounding women in leadership, and the ability to adapt and change the leadership style as environmental conditions evolve.

During this session, aspects related to personal, gender and cultural dimensions of women's leadership will be covered both in terms of "what" and also "how" women can exercise Contextual Leadership and be masters of their context.

Theme 2: The Alchemy: Activating The Power of Self

'Alchemy neither composes nor mixes: it increases and activates that which already exists in latent state'

Being in the leadership space means a deep commitment to enhancing our personal and professional capacities. Creating a strong foundation for leadership involves building personal infrastructure. Developing further on the participants' understanding of the merits of good leadership – this session will provide an opportunity to learn specific techniques and practices that create leadership excellence.

The sessions should focus on building abilities in three areas:
❖ Self-Resilience
❖ Leading and Managing Change
❖ Global Leadership and Mind-Set

By giving active expression to developing women's leadership as an integral part of business strategy we will move closer to the goal of building women business leaders.

'Leaders are more powerful role models when they learn than when they teach' – Rosabeth Moss Kantor, Harvard Business School

Theme 3: The Dynamics of Women at Workplace

The session promises to be a Socratic voyage of discovery with some key questions that impact women's leadership development as part of the learning agenda:

❖ What are some of the stereotypes that the workplace reinforces or disputes?

❖ What are the interpersonal and power dynamics at the workplace?

❖ What are the challenges related to Gender Diversity at the workplace and how they can be addressed?

'The real voyage of discovery consists not in seeking new landscape, but in having new eyes' – Marcel Proust, French Essayist and novelist

Theme 4: Women Developing Women

Networking, Mentoring and Coaching will form the three pillars of this session. Women working together can create a powerful energy for achievement of each other's potential. The challenge is to examine and explore the nature of our engagement with each other and give a definite commitment towards activating the latent energy within us.

The session focuses on both exploring the relevance and

building the skills to provide successful leadership in these areas and also optimize their growth opportunities.

Theme 5: Presenscing

'To see the world in a grain of sand, And a heaven in wild flowers, Hold infinity in the palm of your hand, And eternity in an hour' – William Blake

In this final session the focus will be on evolving the future with actions in the present. The specific focus will be on consolidating and expressing the Leadership Challenges, Develop Learning Partnerships, and concretize ways in which women's leadership will find its Voice, Expression, and Engagement.

At the end of this session participants would have a very clear and definite link with their "highest future possibility" and let it come into the present as actual actions and experiences

The Best Practice Learning System for Women

This will comprise of work in groups in the form of Focus Learning Session, Panel Discussion, Interaction Session, Review Event, Role Consultation Event and Yoga.

FIGURE 3:

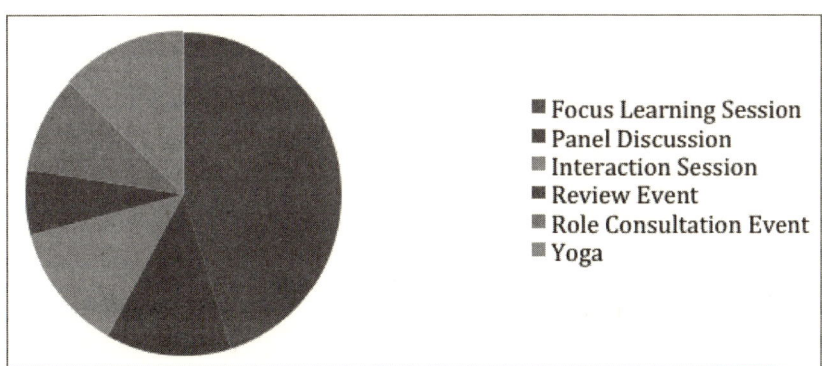

- Focus Learning Session
- Panel Discussion
- Interaction Session
- Review Event
- Role Consultation Event
- Yoga

Focus learning session

This will consist of the participants and a facilitator (s). The opportunity in these sessions is to engage in depth individual learning by each member and to explore views, feelings and thoughts as they arise in relationship to learning objectives, and how this process is affected by dynamics operating at the level of the group.

The Distinguished Panel discussion

A group of specialist/experts from the field will come together to share with the members various viewpoints related to a particular topic. Consisting also of Questions and Answers session, this form will also provide an opportunity for exploring contemporary issues related to Women's leadership

The Review System

It is expected that the members will review their learning in groups and adopt discovering implementation possibilities as an integral process and will also consult with one another to add breadth and depth to their learning. To enable and ensure this, focused Learning Review Events will be held.

Interaction Sessions

This session is to have an informal interaction session with the Leaders in Industry and have an opportunity to interact and explore issues or areas that are emerging. These sessions will be held during the evenings and is intended to enable the emergence of "Outside-In" view of Women's Leadership Development.

Role Consultation Event

Time slots are provided for members to receive individual consultation on specific organisational problems in which they are involved. The methodology followed by the consultants will be based on socio-analytic approach, which uses psychoanalytic insights, organisation theories, behavioural science theories and systems theories.

Work and Work out!

Techniques for relaxation and detoxification of the individual system will be offered in this event. The task of the event will be to get in touch with one's experience, linking body and mind, in a unique way. Addressing the inter-connectedness between mind, body, and spirit in one's personal and professional life, is to empower the self.

Impacts of an Effective Mentoring Program:
Over 600 WILL Mentees

Some Case Studies:
WILL Mentees: Batch of 2009

Following are some of the questions we were asking the WILL Mentees, to assess the success of the program:

❖ What are the kinds of issues, concerns, and goals discussed with the Mentors?

❖ Are the issues and challenges different before and after the Mentoring Program?

❖ If so, how did the issues and goals change after attending the Leadership Program?

- ❖ What is it that you are going to do differently in the future?
- ❖ How are your colleagues and peers in the company responding to your new aspirations?
- ❖ Is it possible for you to define your "differentiating style of leadership" that you may have now recognised, as opposed to the standard leadership theories and concepts?

Mentoring Impact: Case Studies

WILL Mentees Batch of 2009

Jagvinder Pinny Mann
Head-Facility Planning and Management
Bharti Enterprises Limited

Thought – 'You don't go looking for context!
It is happening around you all the time.'

The physical, emotional, psychological, social, technological and other elements that are omnipresent in the universe we live in, create the context for our experience of life and leadership. As we process each of these elements through our experience and learning, we create powerful actions that continue to fuel the context further and become important elements of someone else's context!! Makes you stop and think!

Women's leadership down the ages has been typically analysed from three contextual perspectives viz. religious, political and social.

Only recently have women rewritten *history* as '**her** *story*'.

Leadership – Styles

According to gender stereotype, the attributes and behaviour typically attributed to women are opposite of what is expected of a leader. Commonly held stereotypes imply that women who want to be successful leaders must adopt "manlike" qualities and learn to lead like a man.

Interestingly, studies revealed that women adopting a leadership style that is incongruent with gender stereotypes are negatively evaluated as leaders as compared with women who practice a "feminine" leadership style.

Certainly to be a successful leader you will need some terrific skills, knowledge and aptitude, however, it's your leadership style that really gives your business unit (no matter how big or small) its flavour.

The WOW factor of being a woman!!

Your style as a leader will be largely influenced by two things:
- *The culture of the organisation you find yourself in*
- *The quality of leadership, coaching and mentoring you experience as you move through your career*

When you inherit a style from the culture or are overly influenced by another person, you may find yourself feeling frustrated and on-edge. You may have the feeling that you are trying to be someone you are not. You will do well to remember *that **leadership isn't something that you do; it is an expression of who you are.***

Learn about and then try applying the various styles to find the style that works best for you, your team and your organisation.

Why be like a fish – the last thing that a fish is likely to discover is the water it is swimming in.

Key Messages of Effective Leadership Styles

- *Your style impacts the culture of your team*

- *There is no one correct/best style*
- *Even though you will have a predominant style that feels comfortable for you, it may not suit all circumstances*

There are as many effective leadership styles as there are effective styles of parenting. There is much evidence that no one particular style is right for all situations.

What makes a good leader?

What makes a good leader and just what are the leadership skills that a good leader needs to have? Here is a quick list of seven that will help put you at the leading-edge of what makes a good leader.

1. Accountability
2. Refuse To Gossip
3. Delegate Well
4. Have An Open Door
5. Autonomy
6. Current Knowledge
7. Act From A Place Of Alignment

Seven Truths about Handling Mistakes

1. Understand Your Big Picture
2. You Are Facing A Test Of Your Leadership
3. When Others Make A Mistake Let Them Be Part Of The Solution
4. There Is Never Failure, Only Learning
5. Criticize the Mistake, Not The Person
6. Focus On The Fix
7. Let Others Know

WILL Mentoring Roundtable

While work on the exterior and manifestations of leadership is important, it is even more critical that we strengthen our "inner condition". The more attention we give this aspect, greater will be the self-awareness and crystallization of our intent. This will greatly enhance our chances of success as transformational leaders.

Keep future in sight and act in the present in ways that will create the future. Instead of fight or flight, the leader will engage in co-creation. Two leaders in the same circumstances, doing the same thing can bring about completely different out comes, depending on the inner place from which one operates.

- *Leader does not need to criticize other's point of view in order to put across her own.*
- *Interaction processes are inclusive and are focused towards enabling dialogue, allow space for different views.*
- *Willingness to "jump from the bridge" and state a point of view even if it is very different from the so called "authority" is a very critical aspect since this will enable listening.*
- *Letting go of previous definitions – the shift is also from debating and co creating the new.*
- *Allowing our thoughts to dwell on the "highest future possibility" and taking actions in the present.*

Hence the shift is to get unstuck from old patterns, work with new behaviours, patterns.

Follow Otto Scharmer – Four kinds of listening

- Down loading – This I have heard before and know
- Factual – this is different, the data or view seems to contradict mine….

- Empathetic – I know how you are feeling…
- Generative – as I listen, I experience a new understanding emerging……

Reinvent oneself – Critical success factor

- *Open mind*
- *Open heart*
- *Open will*

Goals – Understand, Communicate, get a buy in to set process based function.

Worked on leadership style

- *Hands on leader –Charismatic /transformational leader*
- Understood from group how they worked around issues

Things that I would do differently

- *Work in small groups*
- *Work in a process map*
- *Let the job value show – as a metrics and data*

Different Approach

- *With knowledge*
- *Method*
- *Implementation*

Watch for feedback!!

The greatest of the challenges in mentoring is the resistance to change and willingness to unlearn.

✽ ✽

WILL Mentees Batch of 2009
Mythili Mamidanna
Dr Reddy's Laboratories
Head – Corporate Communications

Challenges:

- *Life Transition and Starting over*
- *Get back the Energy at Work*
- *Get Seriousness to the Function*
- *Meet and Exceed Management Expectations*

FIGURE 4:

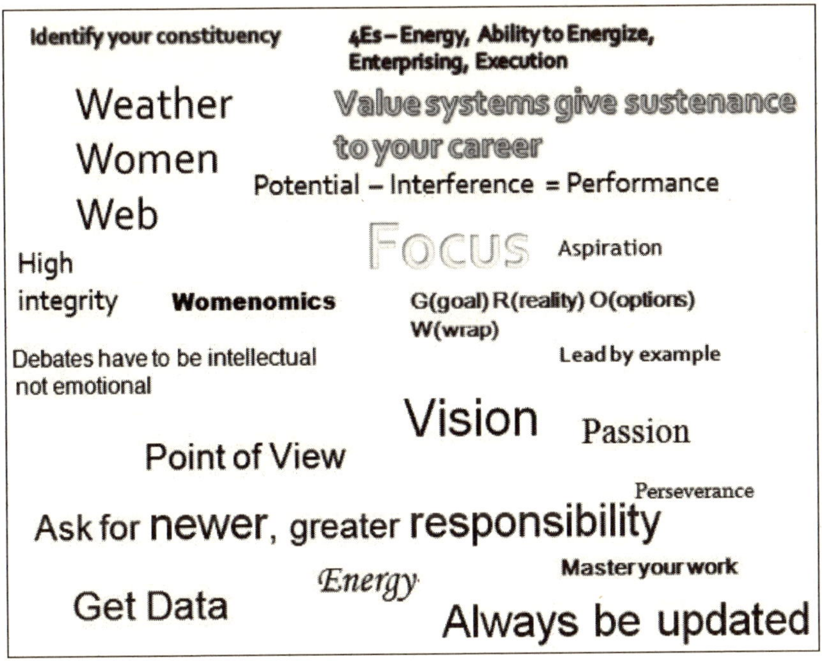

Identify your constituency   4Es – Energy, Ability to Energize, Enterprising, Execution

Weather

Value systems give sustenance to your career

Women

Potential – Interference = Performance

Web

Focus   Aspiration

High integrity   **Womenomics**   G(goal) R(reality) O(options) W(wrap)

Debates have to be intellectual not emotional   Lead by example

Vision   Passion

Point of View

Perseverance

Ask for newer, greater responsibility

Master your work

Get Data   *Energy*   Always be updated

Mentoring Session I:

- *Am I adequately communicating the value of my work?*
- *Am I "asking" enough? – Personal and Professional*

Different approach:

- *Placing data around my work*
- *Time with every senior colleague*
- *Getting more help at home*
- *Asking for more support at work*
- *Fighting mediocrity*

Getting noticed

- *Network outside work but to ultimately help work – WILL Forum, NHRD*
- *Asking questions, Challenging systems*
- *Helping others*

Mentoring Class II:

- *What does brand "Mythili" mean?*
- *Spend fifteen minutes with three people I dislike and report back.*

Step forward:

- *Self-assessment not too away from reality*
- *Finding it difficult to find people I dislike*
- *Stepping up Networking at work … A long way to go…*

Response:

FIGURE 5:

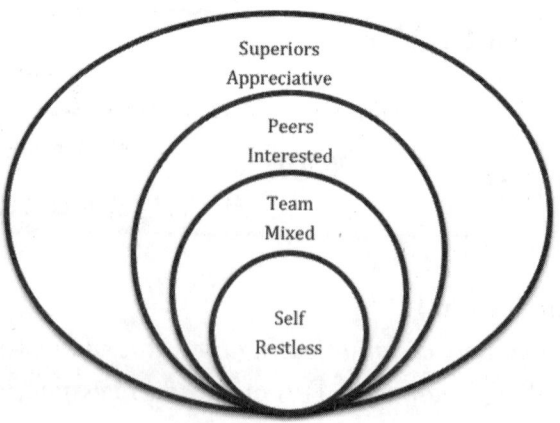

Learning
- *I can achieve it if I set my heart on it*
- *Don't mimic the men!*
- *Work hard, very hard – no shortcuts*

What did not work:
- *Work Life balance got worse*
- *Team seems uncertain*
- *Recognition under the "women" quota*

Leadership:
- *Core leadership qualities remain the same*
- *Execution is different in Indian context*
- *A question one needs to ask oneself – What am I comfortable with*

****

WILL Mentees Batch of 2009
Ratnamala Palepu
Vice President
Genpact

Issues and goals that I discussed with my Mentor:
- *Networking – not leveraged*
- *Never Negotiated for self – never asked*
- *I have been a mentor to many, but never had a mentor of my own*
- *Visioning – Dream, Aspire, Achieve, Ask*

In Business, You Don't Get What You Deserve, You Get What You Negotiate!

How did the issues and goals change post the program?
Get what you want – Aspire, Achieve, Ask

Empower
Build an ecosystem to nurture talent
Negotiate Successfully
What Else, Walk the talk, Work Life Balance
Innovate Continuous Improvement
Network and Nurture genuine relationships

The Bar Just Got Exponentially Higher…
What am I doing differently?
- *Commit to Aggressive Goals*
- *Negotiate Win – Win Contracts*
- *Vision … Foresight … Intuition…*
- *Thought Leadership*
- *Reputation …. Trust … Respect*
- *Change Accelerator*

Reality Check… Look Within… identify GAPs and "Zap the GAP"
1. *Aspire to become part of the "C" Level, Board of Directors*
2. *Build "Trust Relationships" at "C" Level, get a mentor*
3. *Breathe Externally – be visible, make a difference*
4. *Take thoughtful Risks*

My Differentiating Leadership Styles
- *Inspiring Leadership – Role Model*
- *Transparent, Trustworthy, Ethics, Integrity*
- *Result Oriented and Accountable*
- *Collaborative and Inclusive*
- *Tremendous Energy and Passion*
- *Vision – Thought Leadership*
- *Accelerate change fearlessly*
- *Mentoring to Nurture Talent*

✳ ✳ ✳ ✳ ✳ ✳ ✳ ✳ ✳ ✳ ✳ ✳ ✳ ✳ ✳ ✳ ✳ ✳ ✳ ✳

WILL Mentees Batch of 2009
Prameela Kalive
Vice President and Global Head – Talent Management
Zensar Technologies Ltd.
The Power of Mentoring:

'*Behind every successful person, there is one elementary truth: Somewhere, somehow, someone cared about their growth and development. This person was their mentor*'
— *Dr Beverley Kaye, Up is Not the Only Way, 1997*

'*A single conversation across the table with a wise man is worth a month's study of books*'
— *Chinese Proverb*

What is Mentoring?

Mentoring is a developmental partnership through which one person shares knowledge, skills, information and perspective to foster the personal and professional growth of someone else.

'Mentoring is a brain to pick, an ear to listen, and a push in the right direction.' – John C. Crosby

FIGURE 6:

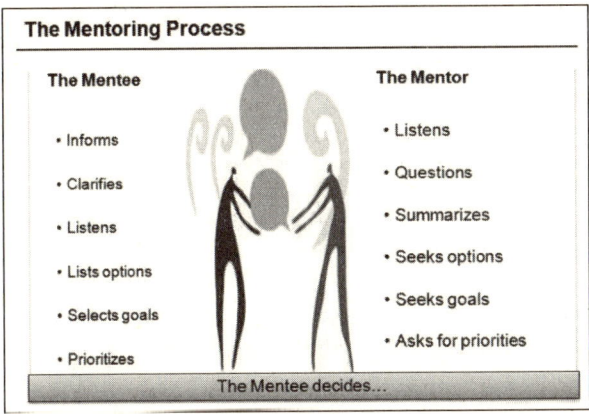

A **Mentoring Framework**: *Empowering your mentee*

Characteristics of an Empowering space:
- **Affirmation** – *Mentee growth achieved through positive affirmations that builds confidence*
- **Choice** – *Mentee encouraged to choose each step of journey allowing personal and professional growth*
- **Trust** – *Mentee feels the process is confidential and has trust in the mentor, which allows vulnerability*
- **Courage** – *Mentee supported in stretching and transforming fears*
- **Aspiration** – *Mentee encouraged to go for dreams and expand to next level of possibility*

Self-awareness: Involves
- *Who you really are ...as a person*
- *realizing where you currently are*
- *what's important to you*
- *what excites you*
- *or where you may be stuck*

Vision crafting: Involves
- *fleshing out your ideal situation ("highest vision")*
- *and describing what you want*
- *or what you yearn for*

Limiting Belief (LB): *belief you hold that*
- *can get in the way of moving your vision or desired outcome forward.*
- *Often either/or thinking*
- *Something that you may be aware or not aware of*

Are you an eaglet thinking, that you are a chicken cos you grew to be amongst one?

Limiting Belief (LB): belief you hold that can get in the way of moving your vision or desired outcome forward. Often either/or thinking.

Turn Around (TA): Transformation of the limiting belief to include both/and thinking.

Growing edge: Your next developmental step articulated in an intention statement and an image. It can be the next process step or the next outcome step.

- *Concept derives from the next place of growth. The precise place where growth is just coming into existence in a plant is its growing edge. That is the place of its greatest aliveness and vitality. Similarly, the place where you will feel your greatest aliveness and vitality are your growing edges.*

What did I set out seeking from mentoring...?

My context
- *Am a High EQ and High EI girl!*
- *Am able to effectively leverage my EQ/EI to connect with people (building, empowering and driving teams)*
- *At times my high EQ makes me vulnerable*
  - *I have trouble choosing my battles to fight*
  - *I carry the burden of passive engagement*
- *Wanted to hone my skills in making inspiring presentations*
  - *knowing and understanding my audience*
  - *connecting with them in their context*
  - *using humour effectively*

✳ ✳ ✳ ✳ ✳ ✳ ✳ ✳ ✳ ✳ ✳ ✳ ✳ ✳ ✳ ✳ ✳ ✳ ✳ ✳

WILL Mentees Batch of 2009
Aparna Sharma
Director – HR
UCB India Private Limited

Issues discussed with the Mentor

- Only WOMAN in top management
- Job insecurity – national as well as international level
- Growth being dwarfed

Observations from Peers on my Mentoring outcomes

Sr. Manager-Organisation effectiveness, Observes:
- I became More Focused
- More Empowerment of employees working with her and seeing a point in what employees say
- High business orientation with proportion of People Orientation
- Improved Objectivity in coaching and giving feedback
- Excellent Time Management

Manager – HR, Observes:
- Change in the level of influence on subordinates to accomplish an objective
- Sense of direction on conveying strong vision of future
- Developing sense of responsibility and train subordinates as team
- With her honorable character, selfless services to the organisation, continual learning desire of improvement never rests on her laurels

HR – Assistant, Observes
- Positive change in perspective
- Increased empowerment of team members

- *Futuristic approach*
- *Better control over emotions*

Differentiating Style of Leadership

'Strong leadership starts with being able to pull together a group of people – who may not have anything in common – and getting them to buy into a vision of themselves as a collective group who can achieve uncommon results.'

My Story

- *Presencing – 'You are the only HR leader who is present'*
- *Emphasis on "what else"*
- *Networking inside and outside*
- *Leadership style with a difference in approach*
- *Ask*
- *Tougher and more Tenacious*
- *Continue to be the best among equals and all*
- *Strengthening "my personal brand"*
- *+ve visible impactful change*

VALIDATE AND VERIFY!
Benchmarking Best Employers for Women in the Workplace

6

Where is your company on the Gender – Leadership Maturity scale?

What is your company Gender – Quotient Index?

How is the organisation auditing the accountability of leadership on Equal Opportunity, Corporate Disclosures, and inclusive growth?

One of the most agonizing discussions that women have to deal with almost on a routine manner – is a closed mindset of co-male professionals in the workplace – who are convinced that meritocracy is the foundation of all talents and promotions in the organisation and that there is a "level playing field" for all employees, without exception. This translates into the realms of paper written as "code of conduct" on equal opportunity for women, but totally disregards the perceptions of the women, and the stark numbers that continue to show that "meritocracy" remains skewed by the selective definition of those who define it – without any inputs from the wide stakeholders who have a differentiating style of leadership. This is the stated policy of most of the HR frameworks and code of conduct – with the assumption that there is full accountability in implementing this, and assessment at all levels that the workplace has zero-institutional bias or discrimination.

However, it is now clear that women define Best Employer Companies – quite differently from their male counterparts. The women also watch with scepticism how they are not being assigned front-line roles, profit and loss revenue accounts, strategic decision making and global negotiating roles, and remain in a "pyramid-syndrome" that continues to find endless excuses for not having more than 8–10% of women at the top-level bandwidth of Indian companies and MNCs in India. In open roundtable meetings – and Open Tea House meetings – women executives are heard speaking in disdain about their position in the company, even when they are holding high client servicing roles and holding large business accounts – which cannot be productive for any organisation seeking its competitive excellence edge.

Companies who wish to attract, retain, and nurture women for advanced management positions in their companies will need to take a hard look at "what women want in their organisations" – rather than use minor interventions to keep women engaged in the vision of the company for business success.

While most enlightened business leaders and companies fully understand the need to address the women's issues – there is a compelling need for them to articulate how this translates into the corporate code of conduct, best HR practices in the organisations, and policies for employee engagement.

It is also time for businesses to go beyond the traditional "best employer surveys" and recognise that the dynamic, diverse, innovative, inclusive, and cross-cultural marketplace demands an authentic embedding of these distinguished features into the Best Employer Survey dashboard.

It is time that companies stopped viewing the whole Leadership paradigm through the narrow view of "Talent buckets" and "people as workers" – but instead viewed the whole issue of corporate leadership as the critical "value-addition" and "innovative-wealth creation" that people bring to the organisation, in a sharp business economic sense that will enhance productivity, business profits, and stakeholder value for society as a whole.

Companies will also now need to apply a clear metrics on the "value" that women bring to the organisation – that is clearly different and complementing – to the male executives. This value is a "sigma-correlative" with the distinctive advantage of women in customer relations, supply-chain management, decision making, strategic overview, rational expectations, risk-aversion, public spiritedness, democratic leadership, collegiality, sensitivity to external business influencers, sales drive – to mention only some of the metric components.

This will now become the true test of "best employer companies" in the new economics – which will not lean heavily on the conservative HR model of "people engagement-reward – and recognition" – but on optimization of equal opportunity for all talents to shine, corporate disclosures and transparency, gender leadership assessment that is neutral and fair, and best practices for diversity in the workplace.

These will be the emerging "Employers of Choice for Women" in corporate India – from manufacturing, to automobiles, chemicals, steel, telecommunications, finance, information technology, pharma, hospitality, and across the board. There will be the same benchmark applied to all companies – by women of substance and style.

FIGURE 7:

Gender Maturity Curve for Companies

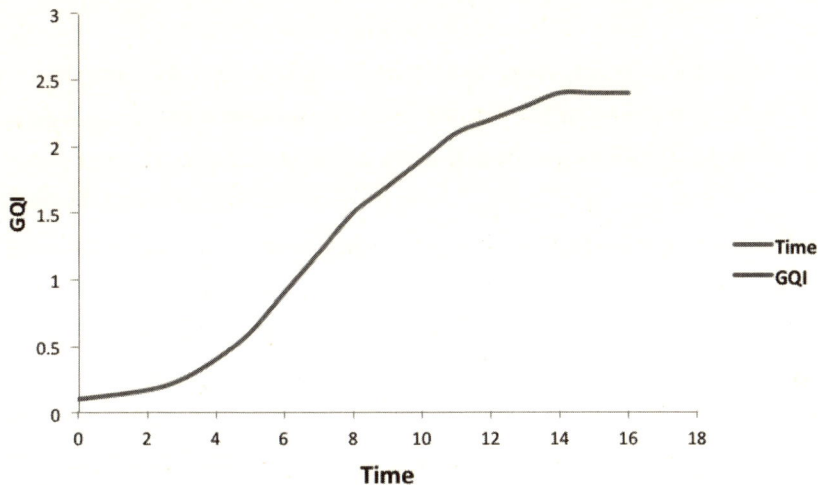

Y Axis: Gender Quotient Index GQI
X Axis: Time Line in Years

* Companies with GQI 0-0.5:
Entry Level , HR is the custodian of cultural transition
Only a "Talent- Issue" for the company

* Companies with GQI 0.5- 1.0
Mid-level , CEO is the custodian of cultural transition
Becomes a "strategic Issue" for the company

* Companies with GQI > 1.0 and above
Top- Level, Board is the custodian of cultural transition
Gender Diversity becomes a Governance and Enterprise-Risk Issue for the Company

The Gender – Leadership Maturity Scale

In the lifespan of companies who are making the transition to building inclusive, sensitive, and sustainable companies – there will be different stages where the company will evolve on this trajectory, depending on the tone and commitment set by the top management and the board.

Entry-Level Gender-Maturity Scale
Profile of Companies:

➢ 20–30% total women in the workforce
➢ 80% of women spread mostly in the entry- and mid-level
➢ 5–10% women in the senior level of management
➢ Almost 0–1% in the Boardroom or Advisory Board level

In spite of all the "noise" being made by Indian leaders and HR heads – **nearly 60–70% of** companies in India, including both Indian firms and MNCs operating in the India region, are still at an **entry level on the gender maturity scale** – struggling with the basic concepts of building awareness, barriers to entry, internal networking forum for women, women – friendly policies, work-life balances issues for women, and biases in the workplace, second-career intervention-type, short-term programs. The custodian is the HR leader – with a mandate to simply keep some programs going for engaging the women. The only real discussion in these companies is about "maternity" policies, flexi-time options, supporting women in their family roles, and related areas. These have however, now become "hygiene" factors for corporate best practices in the organisation – and there is really no reason for companies to continue to stay at the entry-level of the gender-maturity scale – once they have put the best practices in place, unless there is a glass-ceiling management that simply does not want to move any further. Nearly all the owner promoter companies in India – which constitute 70% of Indian business and industry falls into this elementary point – including top performers like Reliance Industries, JSW Steel, public sector companies, Cipla, Mahindra Group, Aditya Birla Group, Wipro, most of the Tata Group companies – would be in this bracket, and some MNCs in the India region.

I made a visit to some of the plant-sites of the steel industries in the remote areas of Jamshedpur in West Bengal, Bellary in Andhra Pradesh, Coimbatore, and Vashind on the outskirts of Mumbai – and was struck by how qualified the women were at the sites – and how little responsibilities they were being given – even when they were willing to do more. Most of their hopes and aspirations die-down after a few years – and they become part of the support and facilitative staff at these sites – with no real network, or access to senior corporate management who can listen and learn, and respond to them.

Several multinational companies operating in India are also at this low-level on the *Gender-Maturity Scale* – in spite of the large strides and high goals of their parent companies in the USA, Europe, or other regions outside of India. The problem is clearly that the "default setting of the Indian male manager" needs to be changed –as John Flannery, CEO, of GE India so aptly stated – and we have several women from across multinationals affirming this – and simply depressed with the low-quality of the roll-out of the advancement of women, even though their companies receive "awards" for their best practices for women.

Mid-Level Gender-Maturity Scale:
Profile of Companies:

➢ 30–40% total women in the workforce
➢ 60% of women spread mostly in the entry- and mid-level
➢ 10–20% women in senior level of management
➢ 5–10% in the Boardroom or Advisory Board level/ Executive Committee Level

About **20–25% of Indian companies would fall into the mid-level of the gender** – leadership maturity scale. This is defined by frameworks where companies are beginning to seriously invest in advancing the women in the company – through "Executive

Education Programs for Women", providing them with coaching and mentoring, cross-industry and world-class exposure, and paying serious attention to the attrition levels of women in the organisation. The CEO takes a keen interest as the custodian of this operation, in partnership with the HR Head who becomes the key facilitator with high accountability– and sets a sharp tone and agenda for validation of equal opportunity.

Companies at the mid-level gender-maturity scale are also eager to benchmark with other companies – in the same sector or across industry – and visibly show their commitment to "advancing" women as a key policy initiative. Companies like Tata Consultancy Service, which has over 1,00,000 women – would fall into this segment – as would some multinationals like MSD Pharma, Capgemini, Genpact, Sodexo, Axis Bank, Thomson Reuters, Monsanto, KPMG,– who are actively recruiting women with sharp metrics, and totally committed to building an exclusive workplace that will respect, reward, and recognise women.

Top-Level of the Gender Maturity Scale:

➢ 50% total women in the workforce
➢ 40% of women spread mostly in the entry- and mid-level
➢ 30–40%women in the senior level of management
➢ More than 30% women in the Boardroom or Advisory Board level/ Executive Committee

The highest level of the Gender Maturity Scale is one where the companies have become truly "Global, Diverse, and Inclusive" – where the Board becomes the custodian of the Diversity and Women's advancement agenda – as an important risk-management and innovative thinking mandate, and an inclusive culture that spans across nationalities and geographies. This becomes embedded in the company DNA and culture– like ethics and honesty – and does not need to be driven for compliance by the HR leader or the CEO, with artificial "incentives" for recruiting and promoting and getting awards for their work. It becomes a business imperative to add women as 30–50% more of the board of directors, and have a "zero-tolerance policy for gender-discrimination". These companies will also undertake regular Gender-Audits of their company and the company leadership – with strong emphasis on the "message" they are sending to the communities of employees, investors, suppliers, customers on their gender-sensitive leadership agenda and commitment. The CEO becomes the "face" of the company policy on advancement of women. At the same time – it does not follow that having a woman CEO will automatically put the company on the top Gender-Maturity Scale! Many companies with women CEO's – have a completely empty pipeline of women leaders in the mid-level, low-percentages of women in front-line positions, and are often not aware of the "best practices for women" for equal opportunity.

Needless to say – there will be less than 1% of companies in corporate India who are on the top of the Gender – Maturity Scale – and we can probably find several companies in the Fortune 500 who are at this level.

Understanding the 'Gender Quotient Index'

The WILL Gender Quotient Index was released for the first time by the WILL Forum in 2015, as part of its report on "3M: *Building Sensitive, Sustainable and Sensible Leadership*" that aims to bench-mark companies on making the transition to "new age companies" that will be "global, diverse and inclusive" for all stakeholders in business. The foundation of the WILL Gender Quotient Index – is the WILL *Best Employers for Women Benchmarking* practice – that is based on the "WILL Handbook:

50 Best Practices for Women in the Workplace". The GQI helps to understand where the companies are to be ranked in terms of their "Gender – Maturity" – and the GQI is neutral to the number of women at the top of the organisation – as the ratio is dependent upon the women across the organisation, entry and mid-level, and the top level of the organisation.

Criteria for Benchmarking Best Employers for Women

Criteria A: Enabler Policies

Building the Eco-System for Women: Equal Opportunity and Best Practices 'What do Women want in their Organisations?'
- Career Advancement Policies for women
- Diversity Initiatives – Tapping "Innovative-thinking" of women executives
- Equal Employment Opportunity: stated policy vs. perceived policy
- Employee Welfare– including safety for women
- Gender – Sensitive Leadership: Assessment and Audits
- Leadership Commitment to Gender Mainstreaming
- Corporate Disclosures on Gender Profiling
- Family Friendly Policies
- Work-Life Balance
- Human Resource Policy Framework
- Public Image and Monitoring System

Criteria B: Corporate Disclosure on Women in the Organisation

Five "Must do" Disclosures for all best employer companies
- Number of Women on the company Board

- Percentage of women in senior positions within the Organisation who are heading P&L, heading a Business Function, CXOO"s, VP – Level and above
- Overall women diversity within the organisation
- Existence of any mentoring program with the level of sponsor at the helm (ideally should be a senior level sponsor.... could be the CEO)
- Any targeted leadership development programs specific to women, and percentage of women covered

Five "highly recommended" Disclosures for all best employer companies

- Existence of formal, written flexible work policy – Including part time work force, telecommuting or work from home, etc.
- Types of leave and utilization, and return rate
  a. Paid and unpaid maternity leave (beyond legislative time)
  b. Paid and unpaid Paternity leave and Adoption Leave
  c. Sabbaticals
  d. Dependent care leave and Volunteering leave
- Family care options like child care, support services, elder care
- Career counselling, Executive Coaching, Networking opportunities
- Mandatory Diversity training for Men and Women to drive awareness and sensitization around issues faced by women

Criteria C: Gender Leadership Assessment and Audit

Across all Corporate Functions and leadership levels

The aim of Gender Assessment is to enhance and promote organisational understanding on how to implement gender mainstreaming effectively within the organisations structures, programs and policies and also assess the extent to which these have been institutionalized.

The objectives of Gender Assessment is to:

- Baseline the performance of the organisation from a gender perspective with an intent to propose an ongoing process for measuring the progress in promoting and institutionalizing gender equality
- Identify challenges, gaps and improvements
- Provide recommendations to address the challenges and propose innovative and effective solutions to bridge the gaps
- Identify and record best practices that have positively influenced gender mainstreaming and equality

The following are the six key areas or dimensions to be analysed during a Gender Assessment.

They are designed to raise awareness about each dimension and should be used as guidelines. The intent of the questions is to gather information so as to enable the Assessment or to prepare a report at the end of the Assessment.

- Organisation culture
- Leadership buy-in and decision making on gender mainstreaming
- Human resources and recruitment
- Policy framework
- Public image
- Monitoring systems and evaluation me

Criteria D: Womentoring: Investing in Executive Education for Women

World-class Cross-Industry exposure for women in leadership
   Allocating Real-time gender budgets – as part of every project – and for Board Positions
   "Womentoring" is devoted to recognizing the important

business imperative of companies and organisations in leveraging the vast talent pool of women executives, and building the skills and capabilities for moving women up the corporate ladder to build lasting and sustainable organisations.

The program focuses on assisting women who have management and executive responsibilities to realize their full potential as leaders – by exposing them to the opportunities for maximizing their professional and personal goals, and developing leadership styles that will effectively enhance their position and status within the organisation for career-building.

Priority is given to raising aspirational levels among the participants, improving communication effectiveness, understanding how gender is linked to work and organisations, navigating the political environment and building social networks, learning to negotiate and techniques of influence, and articulating their ideas and visions in a strategic, persuasive, and measurable way to all the stakeholders. The transition from mid-level to senior-level for women within a company requires mastering new skills set – which will also form an important part of the sessions.

Companies who will engage with active internal and external mentoring programs for women, will retain and nurture their best talent of women executives, and create women leaders who are accomplished, contributing, and with a global mind-set that will add value to the organisation. This will resolve the fundamental "leaking leadership pipeline issue" of companies with women executives.

Comparative Sample Chart: Gender-Quotient Index of some companies in India

The top performing companies with a balance of Gender Sensitivity and Gender Quotient, in year 2015 were the following although they are still far from the ideal WILL Gender Quotient Index. Those companies with less than 20% total women in the workplace cannot be considered for the GQI – even though they may have a high number of women in the top-leadership or the board:

Genpact
Thomson Reuters
Starwood Resorts
Tata Consultancy Services
MSD Pharma
Sodexo
Capgemini

FIGURE 8:

Top Performing Companies based on "WILL Gender-Quotient Index" High on the Gender Maturity Scale and Gender-Sensitive Leadership

Company Name (No. of Employees)	Gender Quotient Index (Components: Women at Top Level, total No. of Women)
Sodexo (33,315)	0.73
Barclays SS (5,182)	0.52
Cummins (6,134)	0.74
Starwood Hotels and Resorts (4,077)	1.25
MSD Pharma (2,007)	0.82
Genpact (34,000)	1.02
Capgemini (51,981)	0.29
Thomson Reuters (9,909)	0.48
TCS (3,00,000)	0.33

IT'S MY TIME NOW!
The Golden Voices of Indian Women Professionals

7

It is high time that we stopped recycling all the repeated stories of well-known women business leaders in India – who figure in the list of Forbes powerful women or global influential women's list – and start celebrating the voices of the 500 million women – many of whom are working with wisdom and skill in the corporate sector and as women professionals. These women have bright ideas on core issues ranging from – building a sustainable business model, how to engage youth in employment, conserving the environment, providing education for the rural sector – but no one ever asks them their opinions on these matters – as they are constantly being relegated to being the "listening audiences" at all –male speakers conferences for so many years. In fact, even national conferences held in India on "Inclusive Growth" often have all male speakers – espousing the virtues of inclusive growth – without thinking of sharing their platform with the women who are key to "inclusive growth" in India!

It has been our dedicated mission at the WILL Forum India for the past seven years –to provide platforms for these smart, hardworking, and extremely articulate women to "speak up" – and **WILL Mentees Manual** that is annually published gives voice to the visions of the successor-generation women on areas of national progress, strategic business engagement, and corporate social responsibility.

Meet Electrical Engineer Vindya Kudva, Robert Bosch Engineering and Business Solutions, Bangalore, India
WILL Mentee: Batch of 2013
'Come hell or high water – I kept moving on...'

An Electrical Engineer by qualification, the journey of my working life has taken me through diverse functions like Engineering Design, Software Development, IT infrastructure Management, Quality Processes, Information Security and currently I am into Deployment of Business Excellence practices based on international industry-established models.

What gives me joy in being a Corporate Citizen is the continuous and diverse learning opportunity the organisation offers by way of training, job rotations, cross-functional and cross-geography assignments which in turn helps me keep myself in constant churn.

Irrespective of the nature of work I am handling, what is important to me is that I stay relevant to the business and contribute to the role at hand as a competent professional.

I have been fortunate to work in organisations that have always been progressive and conducive to employee development and growth. In other organisations however, there could be work-related barriers due to the nature of business, which prevents workplace-flexibility or stringent management policies designed under the influence of authoritative styles of working or even low risk taking capabilities of the organisation.

In any case, it is important to be sensitive to changes in the external and internal environment and adapt, or else, perish.

While mostly my work life has been replete with "ups", my share of "downs" came in 2006, when I had to deal with a difficult medical situation by way of fighting cancer for about a year. The rigorous treatment that followed left me without a voice for some months and even after recovery led to partial speech impairment.

At this time it was my organisation (RBEI-Robert Bosch Engineering and Business Solutions) that stood by me just like my family so that I could stay the course by taking up a role that did not require public speaking or too many direct people interactions and get re-integrated into the main work stream once I recovered.

I was fortunate to have support from my spouse and family to go through the tough times – but there are some paths one has to travel alone. At such times it was my love for my work and the larger perspective of being of service that was therapeutic for me. *Come hell or high water I kept moving on,* did not stop working, but challenged myself with new areas of work and contributed to new initiatives and even a new line of business.

As the adage goes, 'Do not let what you cannot do stop you from doing what you can' if you really want to do something you will find a way – if not, you will find an excuse.

How do we bring "balanced leadership" in India: Most things start with something as simple as awareness? Sometimes a simple exposure to an issue is sufficient to trigger thoughts that can snowball into words and actions. Also looking around you and seeing achievers, is in itself a motivation for trying to be an achiever yourself.

So, good work being done by entities towards such awareness creation is to be encouraged actively through participation and adoption of proposed practices. Success breeds success so we need to keep publishing stories of success to inspire others

What do smart fast-track women need to do – Being on the fast-track puts many demands on one's energy levels and hence calls for being able to balance your body, mind and soul. *Beyond a point, it's not just about time management; it is also about energy management and stress management.* So eating right, sleeping right, exercising right, treating others right and filtering out the clutter and noise from one's routine goes a long way.

When one is competent at one's work, there is no stress – Stress can only creep in if relationships with people are strained. So trying to be a collaborative partner who seeks WIN-WIN in every situation helps create a positive work environment that is so vital to breeding success.

It is important to figure out your strengths and priorities and be true to yourself in order to excel in your niche. Organisations provide everybody the same growth opportunities by way of an open path ahead supported by development programs. If you aspire to walk on that path then back it up with commitment, demonstrate that commitment by keeping your skills upgraded and staying relevant in changing business scenarios. When you find fulfilment in a job well done then career progression is but a happy by-product.

At times, it is fun to move out of your comfort zones and challenge yourself, stretch yourself. *In short – don't underestimate the power within you.*

Meet Dr Zeeshan Amir, Director, GBMS Management Institute, remote tribal belt town of Mirzapur, India
    'It seems challenges still exist to be faced – and overcome…..'
    I was the very first woman Lecturer to have been inducted into the conservative Aligarh Muslim University's Management school, in 1986. Although, I was of the same age group as my students, my adherence to personal discipline, hard work and eagerness to learn and contribute selflessly went a long way in branding myself as an individual who would not suffer incompetence and inappropriate behaviour.

Years later in 1990, I got married and left Aligarh Muslim University for the remote tribal belt town of Mirzapur, where my husband was associated with a carpet exporting company.

The town had a strong business ethos yet it was extremely orthodox socially, with closed view regarding women and girls' participation outside their homes. At that time there was no existing management institution which could use my services, and thus I decided to go the NGO way which was my passion from the very beginning of my life. I chose to work in this remote district in creating awareness about education, basic health issues and productive home based work amongst the women and girls in some of the tribal dominated villages. I counselled and inspired many home makers to identify their own self to become an entrepreneur and strengthen their economic independence.

Gradually, Mirzapur people started recognizing me as a woman of substance having courage to survive and advance a professional carrier in this city. I was offered the post of Director of a local management institute, but resigned after five years, due to conflicting views with regard to the value of the education system, that was operating more or less as a "teaching shop" – rather than compromise on my values.

In the same town area of Mirzapur, I started an institute for offering polytechnic courses in Sales, Marketing and Office management to cater to the youth of the surrounding areas, that was affiliated to the state's Board of Technical Education.

In 2011, I took up an assignment as a Professor of Management and Dean, Faculty of Management Studies at the Integral University, a Muslim Minority institution in the state capital city of Lucknow, and saw this as a great opportunity to contribute to the advancement and progress of the minority communities. Around the same time, I was invited to be the Director of the Women's Studies of the university. Using this forum, I brought up various issues related to women empowerment. However, I slowly realized that I was not even allowed to take any issue related to women without the permission of the Vice Chancellor. All these designation were ornamental to correct their "gender ratio on paper". My voice was constantly being ignored, criticized or dismissed during the male-dominated meetings.

Although, the Integral University has built an impressive faculty and physical infrastructure yet the institution as a place of learning, free enquiry, has a long way to go. A culture of distrust, gender bias, and substantial interference in academic affairs is common. Thus, institutional bias towards women and persons with disability is generally prevalent. Over the years, a number of lady intellectuals joined and left or forced to leave through coercion. I decided to resign and go back to Mirzapur, and place my attention and effort in advising and aiding my NGO to upgrade and scale up the organisation.

It was only a matter of few months that I was approached for an opening as a Director, in a local management institution. Since, they are seriously interested in scaling up and are looking forward to create a university in the area; I have accepted the position to contribute my experience and strength in this noble endeavour

It seems challenges still exist to be faced – and overcome.

Meet Nandini Sarkar, Senior Diversity Leader, Sodexo India, Mumbai

We can see the swelling Arabian sea beating against the shore that hints about how impregnated are we with our thoughts,

The high rise buildings at the backdrop signify the lofty ideals of wanting to make a difference to this world as power Changers,

And the moving vehicles bring in the message that we need to accelerate to the pace of CHANGE.

It is so true ....

We are the women, we believe in SELF and fear not to say # *it's my time now_*

We will spread the message far and wide.. Inspiring Change!

Meet Ratnamala Manna: Tata Consultancy Services
WILL Mentee: Batch of 2013
'Love Yourself, Forgive Yourself, Be True to Yourself –'

When I started my career – twenty years back the first roadblock
I faced was 'you are too young to take on so much responsibility
we need someone older.' I had a college degree but that was not
a substitute for experience and gaining knowledge. I didn't feel
any different because I was a woman.

At exactly the time I was moving to middle management
came the most difficult balancing act period of looking after my
young children and aging parent-in-laws along with my career.
The escalating time demands of these positions kept me often
away from home. I asked for help, mom, mom-in-law, neighbour,
crèche, maid anyone who could help helped me. I am grateful. I
also broke down my daily task list to smaller, manageable chunks.
It gave me a better handle on my day's activities. Working in an IT
company with flexible work timings was a boon during this period.

Over time the challenges changed in nature. Each **promotion**
brought with it a host of new learnings. Moving to a higher level
pushed me into understanding what success looks like at the
new level. I also had to handle issues of delegation, credibility
and leadership. Sometimes I was put in the awkward position
of **managing a team of former peers**. Here I faced issues of
establishing authority and gently altering existing relationships.

The assertive, authoritative and dominant behaviours that
people link with leadership tend not to be viewed as attractive in
women. As a woman I had to face trade-offs between competence
and likeability in traditionally male roles. I managed by modifying
my behaviour to suit the situation. As I developed the reputation of
being clear-headed, objective, and reasonable things became easier.

As I grew senior I often had to work with cross functional teams
to deliver success. Moving from a position of authority to one in

which **influencing others and building alliances** is critical can sometimes be very tricky. Managing **cross geographic teams** are challenging as you need to be very careful leading in an unfamiliar culture, understanding different societal norms and creating a support system in a new place.

In 2010, I was leading the life I had always wanted. A loving family, a dream career (I was the Sr. Director Engineering in an MNC) and all the energy I needed to be the "Perfect Super-woman".

Didn't know then what Stephen Hawkings meant, 'One of the basic rules of the universe is that nothing is perfect. Perfection simply doesn't exist ..... Without imperfection, neither you nor I would exist.'

It is in this "perfect" stage of life that I was "gifted" with cancer, stage two ovarian cancer. Career, family and life itself stopped to a standstill. I stood to lose everything I had worked so hard for, including my life. In this mad search for perfection I had neglected myself and my health had suffered.

In the beginning, when I wondered if the end was near and if my many, many dreams and desires would remain incomplete, I also understood (and it made me really happy) that I love and enjoy my life as it is. I love my work, I enjoy and adore my family and like my friends.

When I started interviewing after my cure at TCS, I was uncomfortable talking about my medical condition as I was not sure if I would be viewed as "damaged goods". But I was pleasantly surprised when the interviewer Mr Kishore Padmanabhan, (my current manager) Vice President, TCS applauded me for my courage and offered me the job. He also made it a point to never molly-coddle me and treated me as a normal person who can handle "150%" of work capacity. People are generally kind, compassionate, and, most of the time, trying to do the right thing. Give people (and yourself) a break. I still recall the sweltering hot day on 6th June 2011 when at sharp 9AM I walked into the ship shaped red TRDDC building and started my tenure with TCS.

TCS was looking for people who could transform "market/ business ready" research ideas to robust engineered applications. I was interviewed and found suitable and hired. My background in building and managing multi-million dollar projects in my previous companies was the reason for my hire as the Regional Head, Business Initiatives. I was the first person to be hired for this new role. It was a new role and everyone was grappling to understand it. Some were also sceptical about its success.

Joining a new organisation and quickly understanding and adapting to a new culture, new people and a new political arena were also very challenging. The following helped me settle down make friends and earn the trust of my colleagues.

Understand the system and work with it.
It difficult and tiring fighting against the currents and it doesn't propel you forward.

It much more effective working with the system, gently steering it towards the changes required.

Embrace change.
What it takes to succeed in any new situation is a matter of learning new ways of working and, most importantly, letting go of old beliefs if needed.

Leverage networks.
In every career move, you need both knowledgeable insiders and impartial outsiders to provide you with realistic feedback and political advice.

Love, Respect and Believe in Yourself.
'Love yourself. Forgive yourself. Be true to yourself. How you treat yourself sets the standard for how others will treat you.'

WILL Mentee: Batch of 2014

Wishes her name to be in confidence, but her experience in the Indian armed forces is un-missable:

'All I need is an equal ground to fight it out – a complete white patch without demarcations.'

I was born in a family of four sisters – all of whom are today WOMEN of the highest order in respective fields. The vision in my family was only to achieve accomplishment for their children – the concept of being a girl child was never embarked in our minds. So, I went ahead, played sports, laundered around on a Bajaj 2-wheeler scooter as a fifth grade child, then graduated to a Honda motorcycle and then a bullet bike!

Already a state level cross country runner, I took immense participation in marathons and short distance running. Sports inclined me to join the National Cadet Corps, and I became the first girl to command the prestigious Indian Republic Day PARADE, at Rajpath, India Gate, from Maharashtra Directorate on 26th January 2001

That's the turning point where I got motivated to serve the country, as in the power that I felt when my voice was heard by the entire world. It takes a turmoil of efficiency and confidence to be there at the fore front and command a national parade (led a contingent of 200 cadets) with a sword drill at the national level. This is the place where I got the All India Champions Trophy at the hands of the then honourable Prime Minister Shri Atal Bihari Vajpayee.

Soaring up in the sky, I took off to join the coveted Officers Training Academy – Chennai and got commissioned as Lieutenant Pramila Mohite in September 2003.

That is when the struggle started – at this point of time, the story of being a women – it all started here……..

Having possessed the superb spectacular voice to command a parade, I began to be perceived as a threat to all Gentlemen officers at the Army Academy. I competed thoroughly for all the higher posts, but in vain as there was no history of a women commanding a mixed breed of men and women. I had to face a lot of male chauvinism attitude – that if a woman commands this Academy parade *it would be a failure for the gentlemen officers*.

I was replaced by another colleague for leading the Academy parade – who was clearly no match for my voice and skills – and the whole of the academy realized it including instructors but all in vain. I felt disgraced but did not give up, and took away three gold medals and got commissioned into the Army Ordnance Corps. I always did way beyond expected of a woman. Hence I had no male competition as such, as they lagged way far behind.

As years passed by everything was fine, but when l I got married – the concept changed.

To my surprise my counterparts already began the planning for me – and started circulating perceptions that:

'*All her dedication will be lost after family planning!*

She will want only spouse postings

She is here just to earn remunerations and have a job security

She is not here anymore to serve the country

So just don't let her stay with her husband.'

We fought for eight long years to get a combined "spouse-posting" and it never happened. I lost the battle here and gave up being in the ARMY – *a bright young women desirous of serving the nation with a gold medallist, just gives up her career for not being allowed to stay together as that would hamper her performance – I wish they had brains to think that productivity is higher when stress is less.*

That is what the Army did to a bright officer – they let her leave the service, without even bothering to hold a counselling session and understand the weak points of the system for a better tomorrow of women officers.

Further, all women officers in the Indian army have to retire at fourteen years of service, and are not given any pension.

I would suggest that a thorough perspective of change is required in the entire mindset, politics, and general framework of the minds of Indian Men. A system wherein women could be put on permanent commission, and keep the system equal for men and women. I do not deny that fighting arms in battle is debatable for women – but it is unjust to use the women for fourteen years just to fill up the ranks in the name of "women empowerment" and then dropping them off in the middle, where age and career both come at a standstill.

Can the government be more educated on the definition of Women empowerment? It is not merely the appointment of women in certain fields and saying our job is done, but empowering the women to the fullest.

Anyways THE TIME HAS COME when the women of India will go into complete transformation themselves as you can see the way they are progressing in all fields.

All I need is an equal ground to fight it out – a complete white patch without demarcations.

Meet Gayathri Ramamurthy, Talent – COE, Leadership Development, and D&I, Capgemini, India

I envision a perfect world; a world in which a woman is as valued as a man in all spheres of her life! However, I presently limit myself to the corporate world.

Economics states that equilibrium price in the market are

achieved when quantity demanded equals quantity supplied. When we ignore 50% of world population as a potential resource, how can we ever achieve equilibrium? What then happens to my dream of a perfect world? My efforts are but a small dot in the investment of time, resource and energy of many leaders on this global paradox.

I have often tried to set aside my emotions and ask myself, "What is stopping corporate India?"

From a business viewpoint, studies show diversity generates more than just economic value. Women bring to the table a different perspective and can enhance the thought process on decision –making.. *Honestly, I refuse to get defensive and validate through quoting research or authors on why women need to be in leadership positions in corporate world!*

If so, why are corporates not doing the right thing?

In my opinion an "inclusive" organization for women is one in which not just infrastructure facilities and safety features are deployed and we applaud ourselves on this fundamental requirement of best practices, but we also ensure a mind-set change across-the-board especially in the managerial cadre. I find it a convenient reaction of people, when they hide behind the term, "unconscious bias". *Bias is an inclination of temperament or outlook to present or hold a partial perspective and a refusal to even consider the possible merits of alternative points of view.* **Are we unconscious when we think or when we speak?**

An inclusive organization will commit across – the – board to ensure equitable opportunities and transparency in the same. Surely, having periodic audits by an unbiased external forum will highlight areas of improvement and enable adoption of best practices.

My personal journey has been cushioned compared to many of my counterparts. Though this does not give me the privilege to look the other way when I see: yes, the shunned word, discrimination! To me this is the core reason that I assumed responsibility to lead diversity and Inclusion in my organization.

IN PURSUIT OF BALANCED LEADERSHIP
50 Best Practices for Women in the Workplace

8

'Ask Not what you can do for the Women
Ask what the Women can do for you!'

Balanced Leadership eco-system companies will allow for all talents to shine – for the optimization of wealth-creation and business success.

There can be Meritocracy only after there is Equal Opportunity.

And the equal opportunity best practices have to be validated – before we begin to place a premium on meritocracy.
   Zero Tolerance for gender-discrimination!

It is now clear that women's perception about equal opportunity in the workplace – is quite different as defined by men. It is also clear that women do not find a "level playing field" and it is time for companies, organisations, and business forums to move from the elementary sharing of anecdotes and stories, and building awareness and sensitization programs – to the important conscious action to "Validate, Verify and Benchmark" – the best practices for Women in the Workplace. There is an increasing pressure from the diverse range of stakeholders – many of whom are women – to question the accountability of the senior company leadership, CEO, and HR leaders who have been given the custodianship of driving sustainable, judicious, and long-term business growth and profits – for missing the targets on creating a culture for equal opportunity where there is "zero tolerance for gender-discrimination" against women, and where "metrics and numbers" will validate the progress in this direction. In fact, it is quite baffling how companies place a huge metric on almost all functions of the corporate assessment – from sales, to revenues, profits, costs, employee engagement – but shy away when it comes to placing "metrics" on progress for advancing women in the workplace – and expect everyone to accept the "soft-speak" on commitment, dedication, and aggressive drive.

Year 2008: Pune

A group of passionate, dedicated and very committed women from Infosys, Satyam computers, Citigroup, Deloitte, Microsoft, ONGC, Tata Consultancy Services, KPMG, GE got together at the evening-bar at "Lemon Tree" in Pune, and started to discuss the "stories and struggles" in the workplace, one by one – at the end of the 5th WILL Forum India meeting. We listened, we learnt, we empathized, we cried, we laughed, we rebelled – but we also kept focused on just how to improve the seemingly "unresolvable" situation, where smart and hardworking women executives seemed to be overlooked by the "moods and mindsets" of the male – dominated workplace. Even in the best companies – the stories from the women were the same – many were simply being ignored in the power play, many were tired of being treated as "outsiders" all the time, many were simply working too hard to get visible, and many were being cast-aside because they were seen as a "potential threat" to the decision-making hierarchy by their articulation and open ideas. One of the women who had given twenty-eight years of her life to the company – grieved all night, as she spoke about they had hired a new HR Head and rewired the company, and relegated her to a non-visible role of leading "sustainability".

That is how the idea was born – of preparing a "Handbook" on Best Practices for Women in the workplace – at a night-bar at Lemon-Tree!

The next morning when all the women returned to the 5th *WILL Meeting* – they were totally set with smart power point presentations on how to build "sustainable" companies, that will view the long-term goal of embracing the talents and productivity of all their stakeholders, rather than with a limited short-term view of "leaders for profit". The PowerPoint presentations from more than ten leading companies women executives were visionary and scintillating – setting out the basic fundamentals of *"Best Practices for Women in the Workplace"* – on what should be the policies that will enable companies to "attract, retain, and nurture" women executives, and also deal with the agony of the "leaking leadership pipeline" for women, that does not allow them to optimize their careers for best growth potentials.

The aim of the Handbook would be to provide guidance for companies for developing a code of conduct towards women employees that should form part of the diversity and innovation commitment of every CEO and HR Leader in the country.

The WILL Handbook was as much driven by the "quiet and whispering – but serious" stories of gender –discrimination and sexual harassment of women in the workplace, at all levels in companies with majority male leaders – as much as by the grief of several women professionals who simply had no peer-group to exchange any kind of perspectives or solution-driven conversation.

It was also driven by the need to create an archival repository of *Best Practices for Women in the Workplace,* that would help organisations in the following directions:

➢ Understand changing needs of a dynamic and diverse workforce
➢ Understand the best practices that lie behind superior performing organisations and not just for mere comparisons with Industry competitors
➢ Manage "Diversity and Inclusion" programs in the workplace
➢ Evaluate the effectiveness of existing practices
➢ Help corporate India gain the "competitive-edge" rather than "competitive-parity"
➢ Understand the challenges associated with women dropping out of the career-path, and breaking through the glass ceiling into top management

The first questions that we asked in our survey of 600 women professionals for the Handbook" were about gender-discrimination at the workplace – and how women can identify them in an objective and solvable manner:

Survey Questions

• *What are the reasons why women slow-down in the workplace – and what lies at the root-cause of this?*
• *Is there an aspiration deficit in the women – or is this the result of gender-discrimination that persists despite policies being in place?*
• *What are the kind of best practices that women would like to see in an "employer of choice"?*

The reality we found to these questions – was referring to a cyclical –syndrome:

Women had begun to have an aspiration deficit in the course of their work careers– due to the invisible but continuing gender-discrimination at the workplace, which they could not dispel or overcome, in spite of all their efforts.

The only solution was to draft a "code of conduct" for companies to create an eco-system of best practices for women in the workplace – and ensure that it is followed with compliance and authenticity.

While companies already had some of these policies and practices to help build a more "Inclusive" environment to nurture and build careers for women – growth is sustainable only if the belief is deeply ingrained in the culture and fabric of an organisation rather than being restricted to just a policy framework.

The WILL Handbook survey received an outstanding response from over 600 women professionals across companies and industry, *on the major reasons why women slow-down while reaching senior management position, which can be segmented into the following areas:*

1. **Biological Factors**
   Ø Differentiating Leadership behaviours and effectiveness
   Ø Self-efficacy and constant pressure to show achievement
   Ø Differences in relation to age and social status
   Ø Differences in working hours

2. **Sociological Factors**
   Ø Gender Socialization – unable to break the corporate male-networks
   Ø Socio-economic conditioning that undermines the status of women across-the-board
   Ø Feeling the "sting of rejection" – in many areas dominated by men
   Ø The invisible "glass ceiling" – that continues to break women's aspirations
   Ø Difference in Compensation and Benefits between men and women
   Ø Sexual Harassment

3. **Psychological factors**
   Ø Emotional baggage carried over from personal experiences
   Ø Women need to be more family-oriented than career-oriented due to pressure at Home
   Ø Women are either too-soft or too-aggressive, and often need mentoring to strike the right balance

Along with understanding the factors which influence the continuing lack of enough women at senior positions in the workforce, this study was also aiming for the very first time – to collate best practices followed by organisations for building eco-systems that respect and retain women in the companies.

When we drafted the "WILL Handbook: 50 Best Practices for Women in the Workplace" – it was clear that it will be hard to find companies that will have all the 50 best practices – and companies will find themselves on different levels on this scale, with different roadmaps and timelines. The aim should be to authenticate as many of the best practices for women listed below – as part of the policy framework of the organisation – in the shortest time possible.

For example, we found that some of the "best employers for women companies" like Sodexo, IBM, Merck & Company, Deloitte – have designated an independent Chief Diversity officer who does not report to HR, but works in partnership with HR. However, it is hard to find any Indian company that has a senior or chief Diversity officer who is independent of HR – and this shows: (a) the low level of priority that Indian companies give to the issue of advancing women – and b) that HR still remains the primary custodian of equal opportunity in the organisation, in the power structure and networks that women are unable to resolve, or get support from.

On the best practices of Conscious Recruitment of women for open positions – one of my first learnings were from Bob Chapman, Managing Director of Deloitte in his office in Hyderabad, as early at 2008. Bob had a most committed goal of bringing more women into the workplace at Deloitte in India – and it was clear that he was going to try all possible means to achieve this, in partnership with his HR team at the office. It was Bob who first mentioned that he had given a clear mandate to his

HR team that no position would be closed at Deloitte in India, until 25% of the applications were from women candidates. I am not sure if he was able to implement this policy to fruition – but it is business leaders like Bob Chapman who were the front-runners of the mushrooming industry today of Executive Search Firms who are being given incentives by almost every top-performing company to recruit women executives across all functions – so that companies can show their commitment to having more women in the organisation. But this does not ensure that:

(a) women do not leave the organisation for better prospects – retaining women;

(b) investing in women with enhanced skills so that they can be promoted in the organisation

(c) building women leadership pipeline from "within" the organisation by validating equal opportunity best practices.

The other companies that are aggressively recruiting women for high –level positions are Vodafone in India, and MSD Pharma which has raised the level of women by 7% in the past one year.

* *

50 Best Practices for Women in the Workplace
A Guide for Companies who are at the Entry-Level of the Gender-Maturity Scale
Segment Areas for Action

A. Enabler Policies – Building an Eco-System for Women

B. Career Advancement

C. Family-Friendly Policies

D. Work Life Balance
Policies Relating to Maternity Roles for Women

E. Diversity Initiatives

F. Equal Employment Opportunity
G. Employee Welfare
H. Safety for Women
I. Fast Track Denominators of Best Practices for Women

A. **Enabler Policies – Building the Eco-System for Women**
1. Identify and Designate an independent Diversity Officer in the Company, who reports directly to the CEO, COO or the company board
2. Creating Internal Women Forums and Diversity Programs – to support the women, as women are unable to break through the male-networks
3. Create a Healthy respect for Women – as an important part of the Organisation Work Culture in the company
4. Provide part-time and flexible Assignments made available for Women, to accommodate some of their family-care needs
5. Opportunities for Breakfast and tea meetings with CEO and Managing Director to meet with senior women in the organisation
6. Conscious Recruitment of women for open positions E.g.: At least 25% of applications for open positions across the company, should be from women candidates, before the position is formally closed
7. Celebration of Events – like International Women's Day
8. Supportive Culture within the organisation
9. Gender Sensitization programs for male-colleagues
10. Anti-Sexual Harassment policies
11. Routine Gender Audits by the Diversity Officer
12. Create a Women's Empowerment Cell – for support and guidance at factory-level, plant-sites, shop-floor, on the

market-fields, and at workshops where women are in a minority

B. **Career Advancement Policies**

13. Communicate clear indicators and commitment from the management and CEO for having women on company boards

14. Provide clear career-graphs for – fast-track women to reach CEO, President, Senior VP, and Board positions – to ensure that they stay with the company and get the best performance from them

15. Second-Career Internship Program for women returning to work after family-roles

16. Mentoring and Executive Coaching Programs for Women – from the WILL Forum

17. Access and interactions with Role Model and Successful Women across Business and industry for developing leadership skills and overcoming confidence challenges

C. **Family Friendly Policies**

18. Full time Day Care Centre

19. Adoption Policies

20. Opportunities for spouses are created – as a key Retention Strategy

D. **Work Life Balance**

21. Flexible working Options – Flexible working hours, Work from home

22. Extended Sabbaticals – Sabbatical after seven years of work

23. Paternity Leave

24. Work Life Balance – Five Day Week

25. Provide laptops to work from home when required

26. Transfers/ Re-location made easy for spouses and married women

Policies relating to Maternity Roles for Women

27. Internal Transfers based on need during Pregnancy
28. Flexibility on Maternity Leave
29. Resting Rooms for – expecting-mothers
30. Infancy Benefit – Additional fifteen days of leave for young mothers

E. **Diversity Initiatives – Tapping "Innovative-thinking"**

31. Participate in cross-industry Diversity Initiatives – like the WILL Forum – and exchange views, insights and perspective from other women and how they respond to their challenges and opportunities
32. Institutionalization of Diversity and Inclusivity standards in the organisation
33. Open forums to discuss the diversity issues in the company – between male and women colleagues
34. Create a Diversity Portal and Newsletter
35. Women Focused Group Meeting

F. **Equal Employment Opportunity**

36. Promotion Policies should be gender-neutral
37. "Transparent and fairness" – Code of Conduct established for Corporate HR leaders to follow
38. Strive to be an Equal Employment Opportunity Employer
39. Employee Rewards to be launched – and Recruitment Rewards Scheme
40. Loyalty to the firm to be an important component of the assessment dashboard

G. **Employee Welfare**

41. Company and Support Helplines
42. Regular Staff surveys and Feedback
43. Department Meetings/Off site meetings
44. Tie-ups with Healthy Restaurants for discounted prices for working mothers

45. Concierge Services
46. Employee Well Being – Executive Health Check-ups, Insurance Coverage
47. Fun at work – women-friendly recreation!
48. Recognition and support to women is vital to their well-being

H. Safety for Women

49. Women Friendly Policies – particularly for safety during travel and out-station hotels
50. Taxi-expenses available for Women associates working late – and providing phone numbers to the security to call and confirm on reaching home safely

Some Best Practice Case Studies

Case Study A: GE India

➢ The RESTART program: Focuses exclusively on hiring women scientists and engineers who have taken a career break and wish to get back to work
➢ WILL or Women Initiative on Learning and Leading: An initiative that focuses on enhancing and enabling aspirations
➢ Flexibility/Time Policies for Women
  • Flextime
  • Telecommuting
  • Part-time
➢ Specific Action [Maternity] for Women
➢ Other policy, process, initiatives introduced to enhance the "Cause of Diversity"
➢ Four global initiatives focused on:
  • Women and Technology – critical aspects to help women increase their technical skills, groom the next generation technologists

- Women in Commercial
- My Connections
- Health Ahead

➤ Work Environment/Infrastructure Facilities for Women
  - ITMS support: Attending T-conferences from home; Log in to the GE Dial Comm. Network from home
  - Virtual Private Network (VPN) Connection: Getting connected to the IT network when away from work
  - Broadband facility
  - Concierge service
  - Taxi service

Case Study B: Tata Consultancy Services

DAWN – DAWN is spearheaded by Regional Councils across branches and geographies.
- Further TCS Inclusive Culture
- Providing an Enabling Environment
- Aid Professional Growth and Development
- Engage through Policies, Practices and Initiatives

Objectives
- Sensitization and awareness on diversity and inclusion aspects, resulting in a sharper focus on building and promoting an inclusive work culture
- Creating a central collaborative platform to encourage and nurture eco-systems to enhance overall associate development
- Showcasing TCS as a diversity friendly employer.

Gender inclusion initiative Employee Welfare
- Employee Welfare
- Employee Engagement
- Employee Friendly HR Policies

Gender Inclusion Initiatives – Special Initiatives

- Day-care Tie-ups   Workplace Parents Group
- Stay Connected   Workshops for Managers
- Reorientation

Gender Inclusion Initiatives – Grooming, Learning and Development

- Be Inspired Sessions   Industry Interface Learning
- Women's Discussion Circles   Programs
- Career Opportunities

Measuring D&I Initiatives

- Dipsticks and Survey Studies
- External Benchmarking

Case-Study C: Deloitte

➢ Gender Leadership Assessment Tool Kit
➢ Dial up and Dial Down policy
➢ **Mass Career Customization**-Mass Career Customization provides a framework for how careers are increasingly being built.
  - Recognises that careers ebb and flow over time
  - Provides a more fluid structure in response
  - Institutionalizes framework/process
  - Enables choices
  - Makes trade-offs more explicit
  - Provides greater transparency
  - Extends the bounds and consistency of what's acceptable
  - Gender neutral interviews
  - Matrix for women in Top position

RETAINING WOMEN IN THE WORKPLACE
The Myth of Work-Life Balance

9

Simply put, the career graph of all women is largely shaped by a consistent lack of opportunity at the workplace. This is not about maternity or perks and privileges. This is a much more deep-rooted concept, one of inclusive growth and balanced leadership – the lack of which creates an environment not conducive to the encouragement and retention of talented women leaders .....
WILL White Paper: Keeping Women on the Ramp, 2013

The most significant way change happens– is when stakeholders begin to evolve their existing mindsets, that is reflected in their changing language, reference to contexts, and how they address the diversity of their environments, of which they are a part.

There is an urgent need to escalate the dialogue for women in leadership in corporate India. By "escalate" we mean that the discussions need to move forward with a "new perspective" and point of view – at every step of the way.

When we started discussing women in leadership in corporate India in 2007, the most important point that male business leaders ever had to make was that the discussion of women's issues was somehow a "Corporate Social Responsibility" issue, and therefore not core to the business mandate. I was continuously being pushed into the CSR direction on the women in leadership agenda – by many stalwarts of corporate India – who would simply dismiss any economic-discussion with us on women as a business imperative. Even smart HR icons like Dileep Ranjekar, CEO, Azim Premji Foundation, which is India's most successful private wealth foundation on charity – till this day continues to dismiss the women's agenda to the social sector, and socio-cultural issue for the nation. Others HR Leaders – have tried hard to "hijack" the women's advancement agenda into the "talent retention and attrition" bucket of HR – so that it once again loses its importance as a good governance, risk-management, and wealth-optimization imperative – and also the "right thing to do".

It took us almost three years to extricate the women's agenda from social sector and CSR – to an important business imperative for innovation and wealth creation. Till date – several women spouses, mothers, and women family members lead the corporate foundations and social services of philanthropy in some of the largest and most prosperous companies in corporate India like the Aditya Birla Group, Reliance Foundation, JSW Steel Foundation – and this is regarded as their contribution to the advancement of women. There also continues to be a large pressure to push the dialogue for women in leadership to the dismal point where the challenges become the "lack of supply of qualified women".

Almost every CEO I have spoken to continues to believe that there is a lack of supply of qualified women for top corporate functions – when the reality is that problem is really on the demand side of the equation. Companies continue to believe that men will make all the strategic policy decisions – because women cannot be trusted with such large agendas, and should remain in mid-levels like "worker bees". Even for the vast number of women who pass out of the MBA program, engineering, IT graduates, communications experts – the pyramid become sharp and steep on their careers – and this has nothing to do with their "qualification" – but has to do with the "gender-gap" that men will not allow women to trespass – under any normal circumstances.

My inbox is full of countless women professionals across India – who have left their organisations for lack of upward mobility opportunities – and do not want to get back into the workforce for the same reason. Some of these women have started their own consulting businesses – after many years of loyal service and stellar performance – or moved to different organisations – as there is no place for them "at the top". These senior women who are leaving their jobs are from stellar companies like: GE, Microsoft, Honeywell, BlackRock; IBM, Tata Consultancy Services, Shell India, Tata Motors, Pfizer – and it is not for any "work-life family" syndrome issues.

At the same time there is an increasing "noise" that is being made across businesses today on what can be done to "support and counsel" women and "bring them back into the workforce" – as if the women had a lower emotional and managerial quotient, and were unable to handle their changing roles in business and society.

The reality is that the women are strong, hardworking, talented, and committed to their jobs – and companies are simply not doing enough to keep the women "on the Ramp". The women do not see any place for themselves at the top of the organisation, which is almost always headed by a male-dominated board and senior management; *there is subtle and overt gender-bias for women at almost every level of the company,* where women have to prove that they have "what it takes to stay-on"; and any attempt to dismantle the existing network of power-dynamics to make it more "balanced" is usually met with formidable resistance from the organisation and its top-heavy management.

What is required to keep "women on the ramp"

(a) changing traditional mind-sets in corporate India and building a more gender-sensitive leadership;

(b) changing eco-systems of organisations to recognise and reward women "equally";

(c) validating that there is equal opportunity in the workplace, which is the foundation of meritocracy – and the numbers at the top-level of the organisation must show this ***visibly*** to the women;

(d) stop promoting short-term "second-careers" as women value their long-terms careers just like the men, that they are proud of – and simply need to take a break and get back to work, without any "baggage" being assigned to them;

(e) companies must visibly show that they are ready to put policies in place, fast – rather than spending time debating the pro-and-cons of the issue.

Thus, the question we really need to ask is:

Are women really opting out of their professional roadmaps, or are other dynamics at play to drive out their talent?

The reality is that women are here to stay in corporate India, their numbers will be growing each year as they make better choices on their careers, and women will be redefining what is now "normal" and acceptable in the workplace – as equal partners of wealth-creation and business growth.

This is an attitude that every woman globally would have witnessed or personally experienced at some point in their lives – women come, women go, corporate life goes on. The phenomenon of off-ramping is a reality – part and parcel of most women's professional journeys – after all, one cannot deny that women do have a unique and inevitable need to make time for the physical and social responsibilities that motherhood, marriage, or family care bring. This is, in fact, almost the natural course that working women take globally at some juncture or the other.

So what's the problem?

Simply put, the career graph of all women is largely shaped by a consistent lack of opportunity at the workplace. This is not about maternity or perks and privileges. This is a much more deep-rooted concept, one of inclusive growth and balanced leadership – the lack of which creates an environment not conducive to the encouragement and retention of talented women leaders.

'Women who off-ramp often do so because of issues related to the workplace and not due to reasons external to work.'

Usually, women off-ramp not due to lack of ambition; more often than not, it is done in a bid to fulfil a pressing need for much-needed work-life equilibrium. This need for a sense of balance, in turn, is more often than not – a by-product of the high-pressure and male-centric environment women work in.

Many research studies over the past few years have shown that talented women professionals are often driven to take a break not just for childcare or elderly care, but because the going just gets too tough in an environment that is not sensitive to her needs at certain given periods. Research has also proven that many women do seek professional fulfilment even after motherhood and off-ramp only for a brief period, with the intention of returning to the workforce. However, few are actually able to regain their positions, profiles and responsibilities.

Thus, the question we need to ask is:

Are women really opting out of their professional road trip, or are other dynamics at play to drive them out?

FIGURE 9:

Driving Talent Away

One of the most common misconceptions is that women get married and subsequently lose interest in their careers. Many recent studies have revealed that gone are those days when women treated their careers simply as jobs until they found fulfilment in home and hearth. The majority of the female workforce is seemingly ambitious despite their familial responsibilities – according to a recent study by the American Institute of CPAs, approximately 31% of women professionals are likely to voluntarily leave their jobs over the course of their careers. However, 58% of this 31% of women who exit the workforce seek part-time, reduced-time or flexi-time roles for the interim.

Further, on an average, the women who off-ramped only took a break for less than three years, and 89% said they wanted to resume fulltime careers after this short break. Interestingly, only 40% of these women ultimately did return to fulltime work.

One must pause here and delve on understanding the reason for such a trend. If women want to resume from where they left off at work, why do they find it so difficult? What are the emotional stresses associated with off-ramping and then returning after a gap? A key driver of this emotional upheaval is the very deeply entrenched male/societal mindset prevailing at the workplace, even today. Typically, many male leaders – globally – perceive such "comebacks" as a "second career" and often label such women executives as either incapable or not focused enough at the workplace. Thus, off-ramping appears to be a perceptions-driven, emotional issue.

Currently, organisations do not foster an environment that effectively manages off-ramping and is sensitive to the concept. The practice of on-ramping is also not prevalent as it should be, and overall attitudes towards the role of women as mothers first and professionals later continue to hamper the growth of women at work. If women do not receive a level playing field at work, especially when their multitasking needs are at their peak, their self-worth will likely continue to be adversely affected, and they would effectively be driven out of their positions. Therefore, unless the mentality changes for the better, women are likely to continue struggling against the odds, which would reinforce their belief that 'there is no place for a woman at the top.'

A major economic faux pas...

Corporate India needs to get serious and ask itself if it's ready and willing to lose its talented women professionals, who constitute 50% of the workforce today, and in whom it invests significantly in terms of training time, effort and resources. There is great potential here to view this problem from a financial standpoint and calculate the loss of economic value that companies can face as a result of women who off-ramp.

From the market perspective, women constitute a major proportion of consumer markets. In fact, according to the Harvard Business Review (HBR) in its article 'Financial Categories Where Untapped Sales to Women Are Worth Trillions (2011)', women collectively represent almost double the market size than that of India and China combined. This can be gauged from estimates cited in the HBR article — women earn about US$13 trillion annually and control about US$20 trillion of consumer spending.

The contribution of women to economic gain cannot be refuted, as many studies have proven over the years. According to the *2013 WILL-KPMG Survey on Balanced Boards for Good Governance*, lack of opportunities with respect to networking and visibility; excessive gender bias across levels and industries; and lack of operational flexibility within organisations are some of the primary factors limiting long-term and meaningful progress for women professionals aspiring for leadership roles. More than 90% of the respondents to this survey believed that cultural perceptions and the social profile of women as family and homemakers hampered their rise on the corporate ladder. So it is more often a case of women being pressured to the point of no return.

Interestingly, based on a recent study by the Centre for Talent Innovation, Indian women spend less time off-ramping than their counterparts in countries such as the US, Japan and Germany – about 36% of the 775 college-educated women surveyed off-ramped. This is at par with the U.S., Japan, and Germany, but the time the Indian women spent out of the workforce was less than a year. The study also suggests that as much as 91% of Indian women want to return to work and many succeed in on-ramping. The explanation for this, of course, is economics-driven. As the Indian market has been growing and is still relatively new, the number of experienced professionals falls short of the need. This tends to create on-ramping opportunities for Indian women. That said, the study also reveals the following:

- 72% of women who want to on-ramp do not want to return to the company they left.
- While many organisations offer flexible work arrangements, more than half (54%) of the women professionals surveyed believed they would hamper their growth prospects if they chose that option.

Thus, on-ramping may be easy, but regaining professional progress remains a challenge.

Keeping Talent on the Ramp

So what can companies do to prevent the off-ramping of women and eventually retain talent in the long-term?

One hears enough about the perks and support measures that companies are increasingly providing today. Yet, it is important to first address some very fundamental changes, which need to become a part of the very cultural ethos of most enterprises.

Changing the business language towards women

First, the very language that constitutes the foundations of a company's approach needs to change. Top management must understand that concepts or phrases such as "second career", "female benefits", and "support" will continue to hamper their true understanding of the subject altogether. For instance, the word "career" means long-term or life-long job and "professional progress". Instead of terming returning mothers' stints as "second careers", organisations need to consciously change their mindset and vocabulary and refer to these as "uninterrupted careers" instead. Similarly, the word "support" is comforting, but management could perhaps consider using the word "respect" in this context – women are not victims of motherhood and family care; rather, they deserve respect at the workplace for managing so much at a time! Thus, women need to be celebrated for their personal courage and loyalty to their companies.

It is equally important for organisations to appreciate and promote the thought that careers need not be ladders – where growth is only vertical. Leadership messaging with respect to the perceptions around career progression needs to change. More leaders need to promote alternate, horizontal opportunities for increased job satisfaction and inter-organisational movement.

Organisations can also help through culture training initiatives.

Just as organisations need to change, the perceptions and attitudes of women, too, need to evolve. It is important for young mothers to free themselves of the often clinging need for everything to be perfect – which is not an attainable goal with a demanding career and a demanding child. Women, and particularly young mothers, are deeply afraid of being perceived as "putting their families above their work". This is where company-wide cultural training and counselling can provide the required balance and clarity of thought a professional would likely need. For men at work, too, it is critical that organisations impart training on gender sensitization, gender disparity at work, and balanced leadership.

If a professional does take a career break, it is critical for their organisation to sustain ties with that professional during the off-ramping period. This provides the highest-possible chance of a successful re-engagement at a later stage. Lack of continued connectivity and knowledge sharing are among the biggest roadblocks to professionals returning to the workforce. Some of the ways to keep the connection alive are continued mentoring, skill-development programs, invitations to office events and team updates on a regular basis.

Another group that plays a pivotal role in providing an environment conducive to on-ramping or talent retention is the Human Resources (HR) department. The HR team often serves as the face of an organisation and its people culture. HR can be instrumental in providing guidance to leadership on what works and what does not work for employees. HR can drive far-reaching policy changes for the improvement of work culture. These changes could pertain to flexi-options such as working hours/days and relaxed maternity leave time periods. It could also be related to the provision of family benefits or training programs for women and men who may want to off-ramp for a brief period.

Organisations can also consider implementing some of the following short-term innovative measures. Short-term timelines indicate thirty to sixty days – implementation time!

TABLE 1:

Measure	Description
Pregnancy parking	This is common both in India and overseas, with the childbearing age increasing and as more and more women drive/afford a car.
	Typically, parking is reserved for senior management and the rest if any is on a first come first serve basis. It is unfair to include expectant mothers in advanced stages of pregnancy in this equation.
	Organisations should, thus, reserve a few parking slots for expectant mothers who are at an advanced stage of pregnancy.
Peer mentoring and counselling	Peer counselling is more effective than a top-down approach to mentoring. Given that "all advice is autobiographical" a peer is more likely to give realistic/relevant/acceptable advice than a senior.
Project term flexibility/ options	Organisations should have a mechanism to factor child-bearing plans into account when staffing/ promoting/assigning large projects. Otherwise a woman is forced to opt out of plum projects simply because she cannot talk about this challenge.
	The environment needs to allow her the option to be off large/travel-intensive/long-duration projects so her pregnancy does not disrupt the project or adversely affect her health.

E-learning	E-learning is an excellent and cost-effective tool for organisations to deploy for young mothers. Not only can talent be kept "connected" in a highly knowledge-driven workforce; this is also an opportunity to offer job rotation to expectant and young mothers.
Project-based work	Project-based work provides many benefits to both businesses and those re-entering. Freelancers don't hit the bottom line as hard as because they aren't paid benefits. With clear project descriptions, deadlines, and compensation, more moms who may be overqualified for a position might decide that they are willing to help out with a project because it meets their needs in the short-term.
Work from home/flexi-time options	This is one of the most common and popular mechanisms that companies today offer professionals flexibility.
Sabbatical leave	At times, people may need only a few months off from work for personal reasons. This is a convenient option for such professionals and enables them to devote themselves to their other goals and also stay connected and in the company network.
Friday groceries	Organisations can tie up with grocery stores whereby employees can simply order their groceries online and these are delivered to them at the workplace on Fridays.

Thus, many companies are already on track to enhancing work culture to facilitate flexibility for professionals who really need it. Globally, organisations are becoming increasingly cognizant of the available talent pool of women professionals, as well as its potential to drive innovation and diversified organisational growth. Many companies are already on track to revisiting their policies and processes to support women professionals – and in many cases men as well. In fact, some enterprises have adopted a creative and sensitive approach to making their environment conducive to diversity and inclusion. For example, Barclays offers support in the form of dedicated nursing rooms and footrests and special rest chairs at the workplace, as well as special cab routes. It also allows reductions in travel-centric assignments for expectant or new mothers.

Many companies also offer financial support to women in their time of need. According to R.M.Vishakha, Director, Sales and Marketing at Canara HSBC Oriental Bank of Commerce Life Insurance Co. Ltd., *'In addition to "work from home", we have a tie up with a day care centre, an international agency, where a portion of the day care costs are picked up by the company.'*

Hope of a New Vision

The need of the hour is to validate that women who return to work are given equal opportunities, and are not relegated to a "plateau" for the rest of their careers. For this, companies need to revisit their attitudes towards women and give them not a farcical chance at a "second career" but a level playing field to resume their great work before they left – to give them uninterrupted career growth and offer them the promise of lifelong careers. Companies must work towards narrowing the gender divide, as well as the deficit that women face in visibility and networking opportunities at the workplace.

It's time to celebrate women for the courage they show by returning to take on professional challenges along with those they manage at home. It's time to recognise their expertise and accomplishments and not focus on their leave plans. It's time to focus on benchmarking and validating if companies have the appropriate eco-systems in place to respect, progress, and advance women on the professional front. It's time to off-ramp Corporate

India from its age-old approach and on-ramp it to respect and nurture professionals – not male, not female, just great talent – and consequently reap the rewards of its investment.

The WILL Mother's Handbook

As women work towards reaching more decision-making and leadership positions, one of the key arguments that they are almost always challenged with from within the company leadership is with respect to the issue of how they intend to manage their home life as "mothers" and professional life as business leaders – both of which are demanding roles that require commitment, passion, unconditional work timings, and a desire to keep the balance of their own well-being.

This standard question belongs to the conservative mindsets of companies that have not evolved and kept pace with changing market economics; the information revolution of virtual technology; new formats of doing business; changing aspirations of women across the world for taking on bolder roles; and the important need for a company as a "community" to provide support to young mothers who are nurturing the lives of the successor and future generations of our planet.

The WILL Mother's Handbook is a response to closing this critical gap – for both new and entrant mothers in the workplace, and also for companies that wish to hire, retain, and leverage the vast talent pool of women – a majority of whom will always decide to take on the role of motherhood at some stage of their lives. There are several best practices by enlightened companies for new and expectant mothers, and for second-career mothers, which allow them to feel recognised in the workplace and not discriminated on their professional achievements and capabilities.

The WILL Mother's Handbook shares some of this excellent learning – and we wish you valuable and continued leadership.

ALL MALE BOARDS
Is there a Trust-Deficit for Women Board Directors?

10

There is no such thing as "qualified women" for corporate boards. Women directors have to be simply "board-informed and board-capable"

There is no real explanation
to account for the lack of women in key positions and boardrooms, except a traditional mindset that does not want to go beyond its comfort-zone..........
– The Hindu Interview, 2007, Poonam Barua

The active participation of women on equal terms with men, at all levels of decision making – is essential to the achievement of equality, sustainable development, and best rewards to business and society.... This is called good corporate governance.....

June 2014

About two-thirds of all listed companies in India have no woman on their boards. Even a year after the Companies Act of 2013 – mandating at least one women on the board of all publicly listed companies – one-third of the firms scrambled in the final two weeks before the deadline to find woman directors. Some high-profile firms – including Reliance Industries, HCL Technologies, TVS, Asian Paints, Century Textiles, Kirloskar Oil, Raymond Group, Aditya Birla Group – simply added the wives or daughters of chairmen to the boardrooms.

More than 12% of the companies failed to find a woman at all. The whole exercise was another grim reminder of how thoroughly men dominate the senior leadership in Asia's third largest economy. In a country of 500 million women – corporate India could not find 1,500 women board directors!

This was not due to any lack of aspiration from the women executives, or lack of qualification for being on boards. Several women across industries tried hard in year 2014 to get nominated through search firms, got themselves certified for boards through elite training programs for independent directors and invested in their skills, they approached several CEOs to sponsor their names – and here is a sample of the responses they received:

Current responses to women candidates looking for board positions in India:
I would like to invite you to the board: but you ask too many questions
I would like to invite you to the board: but we already have one woman director
(Even though she is the mother, spouse, or daughter of the Chairman!)
I would like to invite you to the board: but you may say something risky

The Hypothesis then is clear: Indian companies are looking only for:
safe, comfortable, and invisible women as board directors
    if they add value to the business – that will be an added "bonus"

Is it a coincidence that India's most profitable and most admired company – has appointed a women board director just before the

final SEBI deadline for appointing one woman on the Board on 1st April, 2015, so as to avoid "compliance penalties" – and is it a coincidence that the women board director is of the same caste origin as the other majority male directors on the board of the company, including the CEO

 # Is it also a coincidence that India's largest Business Group has appointed a women independent board director just before the final SEBI deadline for appointing one woman on the Board on 1st April, 2015 – who is of minority ethic origin – as is the ethnic origin of the Chairman of the Company.

 # Is it a coincidence that Reliance Industries – India's largest company – appoints the Chairman's wife to the RIL Board – to comply with the Indian Companies Act 2013 mandate?

 # Is it a coincidence that India's largest conglomerate with over twenty-five subsidiaries appoints only the Chairman's mother – as the women on the board?

Is corporate India truly looking for "safe and comfortable women" – or are they looking for women to bring innovative thinking to boards?

For decades corporate India has displayed a feudal mindset of male dominated hierarchies in Indian companies, where homogenous "black suits" are the "boardroom" demeanour – that is capable of discussing hard-core issues like "money, profits, strategy, mergers, shareholders, auditing, operations" – as if the women had a clear "deficiency" in this important trait required for getting a seat on the board.

This has been further fuelled by the CEO male-networks – where the elite "members only" Taj Chambers and Oberoi Suites, and President's Clubs are fully full of males – dining over silverware cutlery, with laced French-style window curtains, and upholstery of the finest silk, and a "bearer" on personal duty to the "members" culinary tastes and wines – and where I have been sometimes invited as a "Guest". Inviting a woman to these meetings is more like an "aberration" rather than the "norm" – as she would most likely be a "foreign dignitary" or CEO spouse, or a government high official or funding director, who they would need to influence.

It remains baffling how the women of corporate India did not try to crack this syndrome and status quo for many years – and the really few women who did – felt that they had arrived because they chose to play-along with the "boys-network" that they have nurtured and played like "one of the boys". In fact, I have spent endless dinner conversations with such women CEOs and board directors in India who would till this day insist that they only way to get there was to: (a) wear the pants like the boys (b) because they were single and unmarried, and were perceived to not have any "personal baggage" (c) networked with men's-only forums or (d) had an influential and enlightened "male-CEO-sponsor" that earned them their recommendation to the board; and the rest of the women simply "inherited" a board seat as the owner-promoters spouse or daughter.

- *But what of the thousands of women professionals in India who dream, aspire, and are passionate about serving as board directors – from the bustling and vibrant cities of Lucknow to Coimbatore, to Kolkata and Chennai?*
- *What about meritocracy and talent-value of women on boards?*
- *What about innovative thinking and diversity of opinions that leads to competitive edge?*
- *What about asking the right questions – for enterprise risk assessment?*
- *What about seeking to represent the "minority" shareholders viewpoints?*

Seems like corporate India never asked these questions in

the many forums of corporate governance that I attended both as a speaker and invitee for over a decade – with the entire conversation being focused on "role of independent directors" and "auditing practice" – with marginal focus on the critical element of "determining board effectiveness".

Year 2008

I met Shailesh Haribhakti – who would clearly qualify as the "doyen" of corporate governance in India – and one of the finest auditors, leading one of the best performing and most trusted auditing firms in India. Based out of Mumbai – *Shailesh-Bhai* – as he was respectfully referred to – knew almost every board director, addressed almost every forum on corporate governance which was never complete without his speech, and had an extensive Gujarati network of entrepreneurs and traders that anyone would envy for their great bonding, goodwill, and true family relations – Indian style!

Shailesh Haribhakti impacted greatly my thinking and observation on how Board Nominations are made in corporate India – and therefore why corporate governance had no meaning until the 2011 when the Companies Act introduced the law of 50% independent board directors for listed companies in India. Even then, the way the CEO's networks selected the independent board directors, the way in which the "recommendation" from close-buddies was so critical, and the way in which women were not a part of this entire "game-plan" or ever considered by the Board Nominating Committees – was a true learning experience.

During my first tenure as Independent Board Director on public listed company Walchand People First – I had a remarkable four year experience on a Board with an owner-promoter woman chairperson, who had inherited the family business. The Board agenda was circulate two to three days prior to the Board meeting, the presentations were informative, and the future plans were shared selectively. *But more than 80% of the time was spent on "auditing issues"* – and these seemed to be the single most important item on the agenda – which is true for almost every company in India. That is also one reason why the CFO was usually the most influential person for nominating board directors – and most of the independent board directors were either auditors, ex-bureaucrats, and lawyers. Women who were not part of this bustling network of auditor and lawyers on Dalal Street in Mumbai – even though there are a large number of qualified women chartered accountants and lawyers – never made it beyond the level of company secretary – let alone being appointed as CFO or board director.

UK Experience

The women on boards review finds that there are no all-male boards left in the FTSE 100, which is a first in the history of the London Stock Exchange.

Within the FTSE 250, there are still twenty-three all-male boards but progress has been made overall, as in comparison, there were 152 all-male boards in the FTSE 350 when the review began in 2011.

The percentage of women on FTSE hundred boards has risen to 23.5%, this is an increase from 22.8% in October 2014. This percentage encompasses both executive and non-executive directorships on FTSE 100 boards.

Fortune 500

It's 2015, and nearly 5% of Fortune 500 companies are still run by all-male boards of directors. That's the finding of a recent

Fortune analysis in collaboration with S&P Capital IQ on the gender composition of Fortune 500 boards. The list is based on the latest available data in the S&P Capital database as of early January. Despite this progress, several female business leaders told Fortune that it's unacceptable for even one Fortune 500 company to be run by an all-male board.

'It is not okay for a company to have a board that does not represent the views of their customers, and women are influential decision-makers, if not the key decision-makers, in many buying decisions,' said Maureen O'Connell, the CFO at Scholastic Corp. 'Also, women often have a different style for interacting with other board members. For example, women tend to bring skills such as the ability to build consensus and to be inclusive in decision-making, which can lead to be better problem solving.'

It's important to note that 28% of Fortune 500 firms list just one female director. Still, studies have shown that it takes at least three women to enhance performance and governance and achieve effective critical mass.

Here are the hundred companies of corporate India that still have "All Male Boards" – in spite of the Indian Companies Act of 2013 – mandating one woman on the Board – and after all the deadlines of 30th April, 2015 have been crossed:

TABLE 2:

Sl.No.	Company
1	3I INFOTECH LTD.
2	AARVEE DENIMS & EXPORTS LTD.
3	ACROPETAL TECHNOLOGIES LTD.
4	ADHUNIK METALIKS LTD.
5	ADITYA BIRLA CHEMICALS (INDIA) LTD.
6	AEGIS LOGISTICS LTD.
7	ALLAHABAD BANK
8	ARCHIDPLY INDUSTRIES LTD.
9	ARCOTECH LTD.

10	ASHAPURA MINECHEM LTD.
11	ASSAM CO.INDIA LTD.
12	BANK OF INDIA
13	BANK OF MAHARASHTRA
14	BANSWARA SYNTEX LTD.
15	BHARAT ELECTRONICS LTD.
16	BS LTD.
17	BURNPUR CEMENT LTD.
18	CLASSIC DIAMONDS (INDIA) LTD.
19	CONTAINER CORP.OF INDIA LTD.
20	CORE EDUCATION & TECHNOLOGIES LTD.
21	CUBEX TUBINGS LTD.
22	D.B.CORP LTD.
23	DREDGING CORP.OF INDIA LTD.
24	DUNCANS INDUSTRIES LTD.
25	EASTERN SILK INDUSTRIES LTD.
26	EASUN REYROLLE LTD.
27	ELDER PHARMACEUTICALS LTD.
28	ELECTROTHERM (INDIA) LTD.
29	ENTERTAINMENT NETWORK (INDIA) LTD.
30	FERTILIZERS & CHEMICALS TRAVANCORE LTD.
31	GANGOTRI TEXTILES LTD.
32	GEMINI COMMUNICATION LTD.
33	GLOBAL VECTRA HELICORP LTD.
34	HELIOS & MATHESON INFORMATION TECHNOLOGY LTD.
35	HINDUSTAN ORGANIC CHEMICALS LTD.
36	HINDUSTHAN NATIONAL GLASS & INDUSTRIES LTD.
37	HMT LTD.
38	IGARASHI MOTORS INDIA LTD.
39	INDIAN BANK
40	INDOWIND ENERGY LTD.
41	INTELLECT DESIGN ARENA LTD.
42	ISMT LTD.
43	JAMMU & KASHMIR BANK LTD.,THE
44	JCT ELECTRONICS LTD.
45	JINDAL PHOTO LTD.
46	JINDAL POLY INVESTMENT & FINANCE CO.LTD.
47	JINDAL WORLDWIDE LTD.
48	KEMROCK INDUSTRIES & EXPORTS LTD.
49	KESAR ENTERPRISES LTD.
50	MADRAS FERTILIZERS LTD.
51	MAWANA SUGARS LTD.
52	MMTC LTD.
53	MOLD-TEK PACKAGING LTD.
54	MOREPEN LABORATORIES LTD.
55	MPS LTD.
56	NAKODA LTD.
57	NATIONAL FERTILIZERS LTD.

58	NEPC INDIA LTD.
59	NET4 INDIA LTD.
60	NISSAN COPPER LTD.
61	NTPC LTD.
62	OMNITECH INFOSOLUTIONS LTD.
63	ORIENTAL BANK OF COMMERCE
64	ORIENTAL HOTELS LTD.
65	PARAMOUNT PRINTPACKAGING LTD.
66	PDS MULTINATIONAL FASHIONS LTD.
67	POWER FINANCE CORP.LTD.
68	PREMIER POLYFILM LTD.
69	PROVOGUE (INDIA) LTD.
70	PROZONE INTU PROPERTIES LTD.
71	PTC INDIA FINANCIAL SERVICES LTD.
72	RAJ TELEVISION NETWORK LTD.
73	RAJESH EXPORTS LTD.
74	RAMSARUP INDUSTRIES LTD.
75	RASHTRIYA CHEMICALS & FERTILIZERS LTD.
76	REI AGRO LTD.
77	REI SIX TEN RETAIL LTD.
78	RURAL ELECTRIFICATION CORP. LTD.
79	S.A.L.STEEL LTD.
80	SHAH ALLOYS LTD.
81	SHIV-VANI OIL & GAS EXPLORATION SERVICES LTD.
82	SJVN LTD.
83	SPL INDUSTRIES LTD.
84	STATE TRADING CORP.OF INDIA LTD., THE
85	STERLING TOOLS LTD.
86	SUPERHOUSE LTD.
87	SURANA CORP.LTD.
88	SWAN ENERGY LTD.
89	SYNDICATE BANK
90	TANLA SOLUTIONS LTD.
91	TECHNO ELECTRIC & ENGINEERING CO.LTD.
92	TECPRO SYSTEMS LTD.
93	TORRENT PHARMACEUTICALS LTD.
94	TORRENT POWER LTD.
95	TV18 BROADCAST LTD.
96	UCO BANK
97	VALECHA ENGINEERING LTD.
98	VARUN SHIPPING CO.LTD.
99	VIKAS GLOBAL ONE LTD.
100	VIMAL OIL & FOODS LTD.

Source: Prime Database Group

So: what is the reason for the lack on women on corporate boards in India?

From Rubber-stamp boards to effective Boards

According to Shailesh Haribhakti: who is serving an independent director on over fifteen corporate boards in India, and Chairman of DHC Consultants – the lack of women on boards in India is part of the evolutionary stages of corporate India moving from rubber-stamp boards to highly effective Boards. Rubber stamp boards which were the norm lent themselves to a process of selection from a homogenous, buddy network. As most persons in charge of business were male it was natural for boards to be male dominated. As women take the helm in many businesses, the network effects will change.

Quite helpfully, the function of creating the right DNA on a Board is now being increasingly performed by Nomination Committees which are far more diverse and objective. This process will accelerate the positioning of merit, competence and effectiveness of team-work on Boards. May the best prepared win. History shows that in an open process, the chances of men and women rising to the top are equal.

Consequence: There will be many more Women on Boards!

But, what is the key limitation in the minds of CEOs for appointing women on boards in India?

As Shailesh explains that in corporate India, the CFO was usually the chief influencer in Board selection. As a pre-dominant majority were male, the thought of appointing women seldom arose. As social norms were also limiting the availability of equal opportunity to shine through education and top leadership positions, the supply of women for Board service was also limited.

All this has dramatically changed. The future belongs to those who are motivated by the responsibility that Board service entails.

Vigilance, competence, innovative thinking and free expression in a team setting will be the currency most in demand.

Above all a mind-set which values integrity, is happy to be in the path of accountability and furiously promotes "transparency" will be the winner of tomorrow. May the best Boards deliver and the best Board Members perform!

The Trust-Deficit for Women on Boards in India

While all the above is fine in terms of being on the "evolutionary-cycle" of corporate governance transition – it is evident that the feudal mindset of male corporate leaders in India has a "trust-deficit" with women in their boardrooms, and it is this "trust-deficit" among men that needs to be crossed if we are to have more women as board directors in India.

Year 2012

I was invited by our excellent partners KPMG to present our findings of the excellent *"WILL-KPMG Report on Balanced Boards for Good Governance"* on the value of women on boards – at the elite KPMG Audit Committee Meeting gathering of top-ranking board directors– at the glittering Taj Mansingh Hotel, in New Delhi. As usual, there were literally only two women in the conference room of about seventy Board Director participants – and I am sure that my attendance was on account of my being an invited Guest Speaker. Next, when I began to make my presentation – several top-ranking board directors who were earlier Panel Speakers excused themselves to leave the session. It was utterly depressing that they had no inclination to even learn about the value of women on boards – given that they had never appointed any women on their boards as CEOs or Lead

Independent Directors. It is the male mind-set that "trivializes" any substantive and strategic presentation by women – that we refer to when dealing with the "trust-deficit" of women on boards in India.

We discussed this subject over wide ranging debates with Mohan Das Pai, Chief Financial Officer and Board Director at Infosys, and other like-minded CFO's across industry – over seminars and conferences on corporate governance on the beaches of Goa, and "retreat" meetings at historic palaces, trying to understand what exactly is the reason for the total lack of trust that men in India have for putting women on boards.

Here is Mohan Das Pai's, Chairman of the Board, Manipal Global Education, and formerly Director on the Board of Infosys Technologies, assessment –

Corporate Boards today are almost exclusively of men. Society is seeing a massive increase in women participation in the work force, they make up more than 60% of purchasing power across economies and their influence in politics and public governance is on the rise. Despite this, Corporate Boards are holding out as bastions of one gender depriving their companies of the counsel of women. As markets become more competitive, more global, Corporate Boards will lose out unless they reflect the diversity of markets and of buying power the biggest part of which are women.

Increasingly some Boards have realised this and are getting more women members. They are reaping the benefits of a greater understanding of consumers and their differing needs, becoming more focused and more open to greater debate and discussion. Women bring in a keen understanding of consumers, the way choices are made and the influence of prices and design on consumer behaviour how our personal budgets determine our choices. They also bring in a more human approach to employees and a deeper understanding of how to motivate them and make them more engaged.

New age Corporate Boards will be more global, more diverse, more representative, more open and more innovative reflecting competitive and global markets. They will move away from the current compliance oriented focus to one of innovation and markets. Women will play a greater role in keeping with their greater influence all across society.

Year 2013

We launched the *"WILL Women on Corporate Boards: Series"* Roundtables across Delhi, Mumbai and Bangalore – to bring together the thought-leadership of over hundred women across corporate India – to understand their perspectives on why there were so few women on boards, to make them aware that they can aspire for corporate boards, and to give them the required skills, certification, and networks to be nominated to board positions. **Here is what the women had to say:**

Why is the number of women on boards in India one of the lowest in the world?

- Companies in India are not focussing enough about Women on Boards, as a critical business agenda
- Companies in India are not best employers for women – and ecosystems in the organisation do not support women rising to the top
- Lack of Equal Opportunities and Gender-neutral promotion processes for women in companies
- No-level playing field for women in senior leadership positions
- Mind-sets are still traditional and conservative
- Companies have understood the fundamental business case for women – but still think that Corporate Boards do not need diversity

- Lack of visibility of women in high-end position
- Family-run business are fuelling the gender-stereotypes for women
- Board Room appointments are done with Networking – not merit!

What can the Women do to get Board Appointments?

- Senior women must enhance their business exposure and global networks
- Women must enhance their visibility in strategic positions in organisations
- Women must articulate the value of women to boards substantively and continuously
- Training on roles and responsibilities for boards to be launched for aspiring women candidates
- Get the buy-in from the CEO and top-leadership for diversity on boards
- Women on corporate boards should actively nominate more women to boards through their director's networks, as is the worldwide trend

Certifying Board – Capable Women in Corporate India

Although there is surfeit of Board-Director certifications and programs in India – and worldwide, from the IOD, Chambers of Commerce, Management Institutes – most of these programs are attended by serving independent board directors – and provide them a robust network of nominating each other on the boards, and recommending their colleagues for Board positions. Less than 2–3% of these program participants are women – and more often than not – these are aspiring women board directors, who are often seem bonding with each other at lunch, while the "power-play" of the male speakers and participants continues at the premium lunch tables.

I have actually witnessed a woman board aspirant walk up to the Speakers table where I was sitting over lunch to discuss some of the points I had made – and she was actually refused permission to sit by the other male speakers on the table, as they were reserved for the other program speakers! Needless to say – I graciously excused myself from the Speakers table – and sat down with the women participant on another table to enjoy an excellent lunch conversation. I must also observe that the "reserved tables" remained unoccupied through the entire lunchtime – which left me wondering if this was a case of protocol or gender discrimination –?

It therefore became clear that a separate program for certifying women board directors – both aspiring and serving was required – so that women will not feel inhibited to register, and will not have to deal with any protocol of male-dominated conversation. The first **"WILL Women on Corporate Boards: Series"** that we launched in Mumbai was sold-out – with over hundred smart women professionals from the best companies and professions registering themselves for the program – and getting board certified –!

It is high time that companies and business understood that the active participation of women on equal terms with men, at all levels of decision making – is essential to the achievement of equality, sustainable development, and best rewards to business and society…. This is called good corporate governance…..

'The forced repopulation of boards along gender lines has disturbed the traditional order of corporate board governance systems, dislocating established hierarchies of power and privilege in key market-based institutions.' In other words,

having more women does change the dynamics of a board and its governance. The Norwegian experience has provided a window into what might happen if and when board leaders and companies elsewhere decide to seriously commit to making sure their boards are truly diverse, moving consciously from homogeneity to heterogeneity.

A similar "window of opportunity" has been opened by the India Companies Act of 2013 – and while the intent of this landmark compliance may have been valuable for giving greater opportunity for women professionals and executives to be appointed to board positions, the Companies Act mandate has resulted in a disturbing *"Compliance-Only" syndrome in corporate India – for doing the absolute minimum of placing one woman on the board, to avoid penalization.*

No real change seems to have taken place in the Indian CEO mindsets regarding the value-addition of women board directors or transition to embracing the vitality of diversity on Boards for good governance and sustainable growth.

Following is some of the data for women on boards in India:

- With over 500 million women in India, who form half the population, corporate India with 5% women on boards, continues to have the lowest figures for women boards directors when compared with USA and Europe – **and this has not changed over the past several decades.**
- Europe had mandated upto 30–40% women board directors in the EU, and India is still struggling with one women on the board compliance.
- With 60–70% of India being owner-promoter driven – it is rare to find a woman CEO of large companies in India, unless she has inherited a family-owned business. The few women CEOs who stand out as accomplished professionals is a reminder that there are only a handful of them –!

- There is not a single woman in the highest paid executives list in corporate India.
- Over 20 – 70% of the women executives remain in the "mid-level" of the companies throughout their career-life, according to the WILL Forum survey. With over 800 board seats required to be filled by April 2015 – there is no evidence of companies in India looking into this talent pool – and simply looking for window-dressing through search firms.

Unfortunately, **the Indian Companies Act 2013, has not made any change in the mind-sets of the male-dominated Indian corporate boards** – who continue to find "excuses" for not placing high-achieving and accomplished women professionals on boards – and recycling the same stereotype arguments that have acted as "invisible barriers" to women getting on to board director positions in the first place.

Following are some of the impacts of the Companies Act 2013 so far – and the continuing "negative myths" that are active in corporate India:

1. 70% of the largest Indian businesses are family –owned, including Aditya Birla Group, Reliance Industries, Mahindra Group, Airtel, Piramal group, Jindal Steel, Vedanta, Godrej Industries, Bajaj Group, Wipro Industries, HCL Technologies, RPG Group, Avantha Holdings.

Most of them have recently *nominated the CEO's/ Chairman's wives, mothers, daughters, and daughters-in-law on their corporate boards, to fulfil the Indian Companies Act "one-women on boards" mandate.*

This is totally contrary to the whole concept of bringing women on boards to harness the benefits of "diversity" – and bring new leadership skills, new perspectives, and new innovation to the company boards.

The Indian Companies Act should have clearly mandated companies to appoint at least one "independent woman director" – as that would have been more in-keeping with moving towards good governance on boards.

2. The same corporate male business leaders who never appointed women on their boards for the past several years – are continuing to lament that there is a lack of qualified women for boards, and there is no pipeline of good women directors available.

This is clearly the same outdated argument being recycled, as corporate boards in India continue to look for "clones" for their boards, and do not embrace the vitality, wealth-creation and innovative thinking that different leadership styles can bring to enhancing the quality and richness of their businesses.

Nearly 40–50% of the graduates from law, medicine, management, PhD's are women in India – and they are equally qualified for boards as their male counterparts, and fully versed in business strategy

3. Indian corporate boards continue to remain in the "comfort zone" syndrome – and hesitate from appointing women directors, as women are an "unknown" component, and may not always play the "game". Women are also often likely to ask the right questions in the interest of stakeholder transparency and due-diligence – which is not seen as an "asset" by Indian CEOs and directors.

In fact, a group of Indian CEOs and board directors have gone on record in the press – to say that they are looking for women who the "board will be comfortable" with.

However, *the real meaning of "diversity" is to get comfortable with the "difference"* – so clearly the Indian CEOs are still on the "compliance" waive-length and have not yet graduated to understanding the benefits and rewards of "celebrating the gender-differences".

4. The only group that seems to be making good money from the Indian Companies Act are the executive "search-firms" who are scrambling to find women board directors – from the same box of fifteen to twenty candidates that they have been using for the past ten years.

#5. WILL Survey has shown that senior women professionals still seem to be rejected for board positions in India, because they are seen as 'too aggressive and ask too many questions.' Many senior women professionals have gone on record on this statement, and boards are only looking for "passive women directors" in corporate India.

In the bottom line:

The focus needs to shift away from the excessive terminology being used in India and worldwide on Directors "board-qualification" or Directors being "board-ready" – to Directors being "Board-capable"!

Women and men are equally qualified to be on corporate boards – as the core "fiduciary responsibilities" for board directors that comprise of care, trust, and transparency for stakeholders – is equally present or not present in the DNA of the board candidates, irrespective of gender.

Where men "seem" to be more qualified for board director positions due to their "experience" from serving on other corporate boards – women bring "fresh, diverse and different" perspective to the boards.

BALANCED BOARDS FOR GOOD GOVERNANCE
Diverse, Inclusive, Balanced, Sustainable, and Resilient

11

It's not about women – it's about enterprise risk management!

Balanced Boards are not necessarily better – they are about being different

It is this "difference" that leads to creative thinking, innovation, and gives the Board and company the competitive edge, and enterprise risk management – that the economist Joseph Schumpeter, who illustrated the theory of "Creative Destruction" was referring to when he said 'entrepreneurship is innovation.'

Year 2013

With the increasing geo-political volatility and unprecedented diversity of stakeholders, future generations will be looking for new formats of workspaces and new styles of leadership – that will be distinctly different from how we have known businesses and enterprises to succeed, and how we have defined corporate boards to function for delivering good governance to its stakeholders.

In fact, the very role and identity of stakeholders will be evolving in mature companies and societies – and those who do not keep pace with this compelling transition of ideas, respect for differences, and participating in "collective goals" – will be left without the competitive edge of the yet undefined future markets, consumers, and style of business access and acumen.

With this transition in mind – it is critical for corporate India to open a substantive and candid dialogue on the key components of good governance that are now being redefined by visionary corporate boards who are preparing a clear vision for being "different", "inclusive", "balanced", "sustainable" and "resilient".

And as women form about 50% of the global population and the present pool of innovative ideas, intelligence, leadership intuition, strategic perspectives, and unexplored talent domains – companies that do not recognise their participation for balanced boards will be putting their shareholders and stakeholders at business-risk, for future sustainability and wealth-creation.

We decided to bring out a report on "*Balanced Boards for Good Governance*" in partnership with KPMG – and the survey on this report brought out that while majority of corporate Indian business leaders understand that women need to be brought onto corporate boards, they are simply unable to provide clear reasons for the dismal number of less than 5% of women on corporate boards in India – when there are 500 million women in India today! The reality is that – while meritocracy is accepted as the foundation of board nominations, the definition of "meritocracy" itself needs to be changed, as those who have traditionally defined meritocracy for the past century have themselves become outdated in the overwhelming pace of transition of minds, hearts, and communities.

In fact, it is worth reflecting – that in the many sheets of paper and regulation that have been devoted to streamlining corporate governance – there has been no mention of "inclusivity." This will be a key component of the fundamentals of the democratic process that ensures equal "voice" in the tenets of free markets, which are the hallmarks of the Adam Smith definition of "free markets and business enterprise".

In a dynamic and highly volatile global economy – Indian companies are clearly not measuring the enterprise risk of lack of gender-diversity on their decision-making and leadership processes – that still rely heavily on financial and legal accounting style of corporate governance, that now belongs to the pre-Lehman Brothers era. The new global economy will reward competitiveness that is virtual, flexible, agile, empowering, inclusive, sensitized, intelligent, creative – and uses all its time, energy, and resources to the fullest potential.

Companies will also now need to apply a clear metrics on the "value" that women bring to the organisation – that is clearly different and complementing – to the male executives. This value is a "sigma-correlative" with the distinctive advantage of women in customer relations, supply-chain management, decision making, strategic overview, rational expectations, risk-aversion, public spiritedness, democratic leadership, collegiality, sensitivity to external business influencers, sales drive – to mention only some of the metric components.

Diversity For Balanced Boards

Truly... so much has evolved in the world we live in. Yet, nothing much has changed. Pressures on business earnings; incentives to "manage revenues"; keeping up with rising employee expectations, risks defined by new customers; non-financial risks arising from volatile markets; changing customer priorities – all continue to be part of the dynamics of the changing and highly competitive economies. At the same time, the impacts of fast emerging markets, new strategic alliances, increasing standards of compliance and disclosures, homogeneous board director profiles, failure to exercise oversight by gatekeepers – prevails as the status quo across business, industry, and enterprises worldwide.

It is therefore time for a sharp reflection, that perhaps a different type of corporate governance – or corporate boardroom dynamics – with increased representation of diverse stakeholders, including women on boards – could lead to more well-rounded and improved decision making and effective governance process.

Women as leaders are known to exhibit certain distinctive qualities that add unique value and complement healthy diversity to company boards. These are manifested as a greater focus on public-spiritedness, better communications within the group, more rational decision making, greater transparency of actions, and a clear consciousness toward community enhancement and sustainability of the organisation. Women are also known to be risk-averse, exercising strategy with a judicious sense of disbursement of wealth, and with greater rational foresight for future opportunities of business.

However, the key to bringing diversity on boards will be based on the organisation's capacity to leverage the differential qualities and vision – that will be necessary to steer the company through diverse global strategies, different cultural dimensions, global mindsets, and responses to innovative thinking – in an unprecedented and unpredictable global business environment.

So, what is Good Corporate Governance – and what are Balanced Boards?

Balanced boards are those that offer equal opportunity across the talent pool to find unbiased and neutral assessments for seeking representation on the entity's corporate board of directors. It does not designate an "equal number" of men or women or any other stakeholder value; however, it clearly shows that there is equal opportunity for all diverse stakeholders to present their nominations for board positions, in a transparent and clear corporate disclosures best practices format.

Under the traditional umbrella of corporate governance, that dominates the conservative thinking of most of corporate India, European corporate law, and Wall Street – the key components are defined as the fundamentals of determining board effectiveness, being custodians of the faith and trust of the company's diverse shareholders, disbursing the fiduciary responsibilities of board directors, and steering the company with strategic vision and transparent disclosures.

In the newer dynamics and demographics of the business matrix – that looks like a kaleidoscope of vastly diverse customers, suppliers, investors, employees, and stakeholders – companies will need to make space for adding the terms "diversity" and "inclusivity" – in defining "good corporate governance".

How does this translate into Increased representation of women in the board room = strengthened governance and returns?

Despite the paucity of any kind of comparable data for diversity and business performance on corporate boards, it is possible to find some correlations. In other words, there is available data to validate that companies with more gender-diverse boards perform significantly better financially than those with less gender-diverse boards.

What constitutes the "critical mass" of women on corporate boards?

If an increased number of women directors can effect improvement in financial performance, how many more will make a difference? Is there a critical mass that can bring significant change to the boardroom?

In their 2007 studies, both Catalyst and McKinsey pinpointed 30% – or three or more women – as a crucial figure where women's representation made a significant impact on the bottom line of a company. The McKinsey report considered the performance of companies with various numbers of women on the board and found that the largest gap in performance existed between those companies with no female directors and those with three or more on their board.

(*McKinsey and Company, Women Matter: Gender Diversity, A Corporate Performance Driver, October 2007*).

Another study by the Conference Board of Canada found that companies with two or more women on their boards of directors in1995 were more likely to have higher revenues and profits six years later in 2001.

(*Conference Board of Canada. Women on Boards: Not just the Right Thing … But the "Bright" Thing," May 2002*)

A similar conclusion was reached through a joint research project from the Richard Ivey School of Business in Canada and the Wellesley Centres for women in the US: 'While a lone women can and often does make substantial contributions, and two women are generally more powerful than one, increasing the number of women to three or more enhances the likelihood that women's voices are heard and that boardroom dynamics change substantially.'

"Critical Mass on Corporate Boards:
Why Three of More Women Enhance Governance." Wellesley Centres for Women, Executive Summary, 2006.

The critical mass of women directors is good for corporate governance in at least three ways, according to their research:

1. The content of boardroom discussion is more likely to include the perspectives of the multiple stakeholders who affect, and

are affected by, company performance – not only shareholders, but also employees, customers, suppliers and the community at large.

2. Difficult issues and problems are considerably less likely to be ignored or brushed aside, which strengthens decision making.

3. Boardroom dynamics are more open and collaborative, which helps management hear the board's concerns and take them to heart without defensiveness.

   (Kramer, Vicki W., Alison M. Konrad, and Sumru Erkut." Critical Mass on Corporate Boards: Why Three of More Women Enhance Governance." Wellesley centres for Women.

The 30% Club in UK

The 30% Club was launched in 2009 in the UK – with the aim of bringing gender equality at corporate board levels, targeting 30% women on boards by 2015. Helena Morrisey, founder of the 30% Club in the UK says, 'Our belief is that, as more women join boards without the imposition of quotas, the more they can demonstrate the value they can add. By the time we get to 30%, the system will be self-perpetuating,' The reason for advocating 30% is that it seems an optimum standard as the representation of women is far too low at the corporate level to aim for a higher standard. A goal of 30% seems right to various organisations as a drastic jump to 50% does not appear realistic. In the *2015 Women in P&U Index (Power and Utilities Index)*, EY analysed the top 200 utilities to determine who had the most women in positions of influence on the board and the senior management team. Overall, women only constituted 5% of board directors, 17% of non-executive directors, 14% of board members and 13% of senior management teams.

The 30% Club is increasingly considering overall board

effectiveness including diversity as an important aspect of good governance. The members of 30% Club are Chairs, CEOs or the equivalent at companies and organisations, who are working to fulfil the goals of the 30% Club and have committed to recruiting other Chairs to support its mission. Since 2014, the 30% Club also have a mentoring scheme, that offers cross-company, cross-sector mentoring to mid-career women. It aims to complement other schemes within individual organisations or in the marketplace, where cross-company mentoring is usually only available to very senior women. This is a part of 30% Club initiatives aimed at helping to develop a broader pipeline of women and "balance the pyramid" at all levels.

As per the Lord Davies Report 2015 in UK Parliament, there are more women than ever before on British boards. Now there is little need to set out the business case, the role women are playing at the top table and the women themselves are selling itself and casting a bright light down into the business. According to the Report, there is no shortage of talented and aspiring women, so reaching the target of 30% should not be a difficult task. The voluntary compliance by firms was seen as doubtful but the Report argues that it has been successful.

Has the Business Case for Diverse Boards had any impact?

If impact is measured in terms of promoting others to examine the business case argument, then clearly, the Catalyst and McKinsey reports, whose results were highly publicized, resulted in similar research being undertaken in other countries. In addition, these reports became benchmarks for the validity of this argument. Whether in Hong Kong or France, their findings were quoted to buttress the call for more action, as mentioned above in Australia, or to support pending policy proposals as in France when quota legislation was being deliberated.

If impact is determined by what policies emerge to address the paucity of women directors, then the coinciding release of reports connecting board diversity with increased profitability with the introduction of quota laws within the very same countries is indeed fortuitous. Clearly, the various country studies mentioned above provided data that supported the move of policy makers to mandate a percentage of board seats to be allocated for women in Europe.

If impact is measured by the responsiveness of a large group of global companies improving their percentage of women's representation on corporate boards, the business case has not been heard sufficiently. The bottom line impact of women directors is a powerful line of reasoning supported by copious research already, but it needs to be repeated by the media, advocates, corporate governance groups and shareholders for corporate leaders to listen.

Further, while current research is substantial, additional research needs to be conducted in countries where such data does

FIGURE 10:

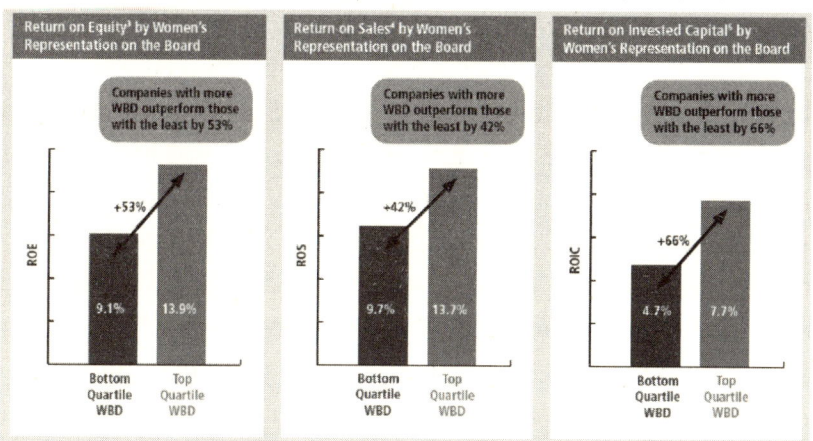

Source: *2007 of Corporate Performance of Fortune 500 Companies and Women's Representation on Boards*

not exist. All of these studies reinforce each other and perhaps, through sheer volume, the message may begin to penetrate boardrooms and executive suites.

In fact, several arguments dispel the myth that women are incapable of performing on corporate boards, or do not have the required "qualification" – or are not "board-ready"

- The majority of male directors appointed to corporate boards in India actually have never had any previous board experience – and there seems to be no requirement for them to get any "qualifications" for being board-ready.
- Clearly, this stems from the unconscious bias that women executives need something "more" than their male counterparts to be of value to the corporate boards – which in itself is a fallacy that needs to be dismissed as more women learn to ask, compete, nominate, and exercise their right to be on the boards, as equal partners of the wealth-creation process of the enterprises.

It is indeed the right time to do away with the stereotype board director profile and find ways to integrate the demands of markets and investors, and redefine the profile of board directors for nominating committees and CEOs.

While the idea is not to propagate that balanced boards are better, they are certainly different and hold the potential to strengthen corporate governance by diffusing the influence of the dominant majority of boards – to bring innovative thinking to business strategy. However, it is equally important for women to take initiatives to position themselves as strong and authentic contenders for corporate board director positions. They need to visibly exhibit a sense of mission, passion and a commitment to make a difference to the vision, strategy, and wealth-creation of the organisation. Further, women need to consciously find the right platforms, networks and board nominating committees to complete their journey to the corporate boardroom.

From the market perspective, women constitute a major proportion of consumer markets. In fact, according to Harvard Business Review (HBR), women collectively represent almost double the market size than that of India and China combined. This can be gauged from estimates that women earn about USD 13 trillion annually and control about USD 20 trillion of consumer spending, which is expected to record more than 38% growth each to USD 18 trillion and to USD 28 trillion, respectively.

The labour pool argument for women on boards seems to be the strongest, as the representation of women in the total workforce is significant and on the rise – there are 500 million women in India presently, and women constitute 8% of the global population. Perceivable career growth up to board level helps retain women employees.

'We need women in leadership positions not only because they can manage as well as men but because they manage differently than men. We need them because they tend to – over time and in the aggregate – make different kinds of decisions and bring different ideas to the table. We need women who will approach risk from a different perspective, who take an altered view of time and conflict, and who understand diversity as something more than an abstract theory. We need women who operate as managers, not just as employees or critics; who are as competitive for themselves as they are for their children. And we need more men to recognise that having women around the table isn't just a nice thing to do. It makes for a better table.'

Amid prevailing uncertain economic times on the one hand – and an evolving social landscape on the other – India's corporate world is poised at significant crossroads; and at this juncture, it's time to embrace change for true progress within organisations – change towards "balanced leadership".

What is holding back corporate India from balanced leadership at decision-making positions? One possible reason maybe that the concepts of "diversity for balanced leadership" and general "gender equality" at the workplace have for long been interlinked. Many leaders across companies are quick to lay the blame on the lack of "available" and experienced women professionals for leadership roles in the Indian corporate pipeline.

However, a large population of women executives believe that this boils down to an "uneven playing field", along with pre-conceived perceptions around women and their long-term commitment to high-stress front-line jobs. Lack of opportunities with respect to networking and visibility; excessive gender bias across levels and industries; and lack of operational flexibility within organisations – are some of the primary factors limiting long-term and meaningful progress for women professionals aspiring for leadership roles. *The WILL-KPMG 2013 survey reinforces* this – more than 90% of the respondents believe that cultural perceptions and the social profile of women as family and homemakers hamper their rise on the corporate ladder. Further, more than 75% agree that visibility and networks available for women to be nominated for Corporate Board positions is still completely inadequate.

For this, it has become imperative that the subject of diversity in corporate boards is delinked from themes of women's emancipation. It is the compelling economic rewards of "balanced leadership" that generates the need for healthy diversity to strengthen good corporate governance.

A view of the top 200 blue-chip companies listed on the Bombay Stock Exchange (BSE-200) gives a startling assessment of just how skewed the situation is with regard to available board seats

FIGURE 11:

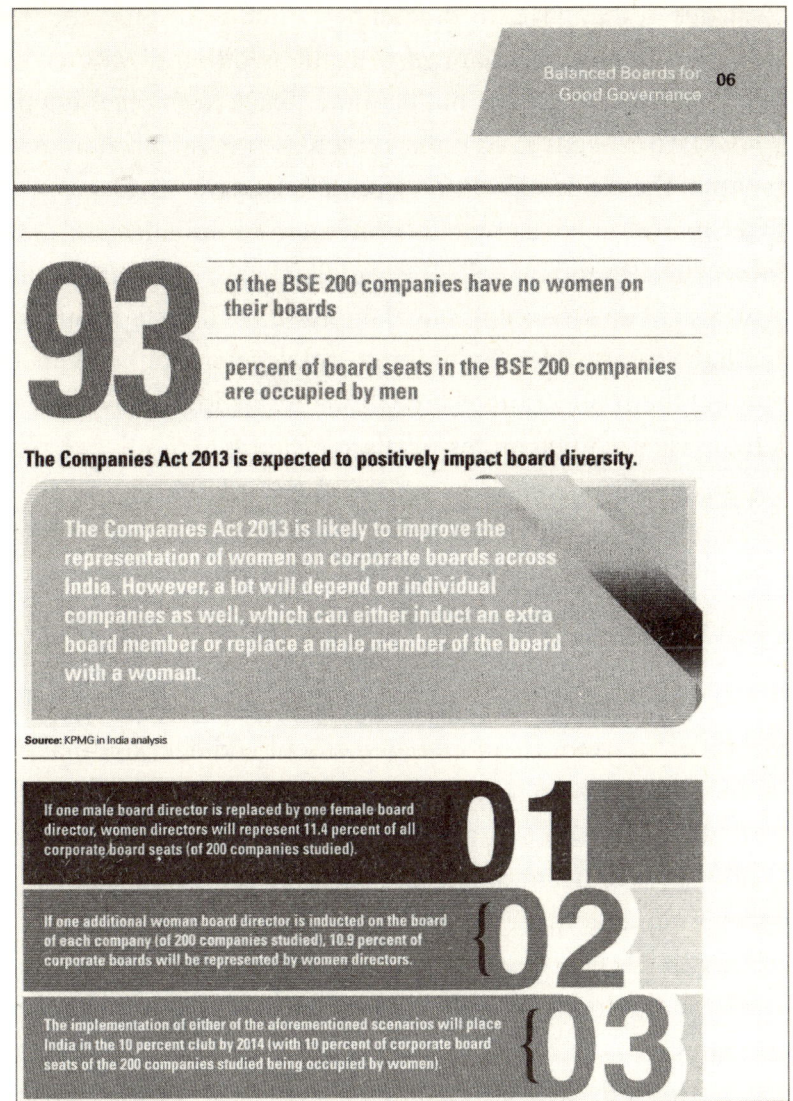

The Companies Bill 2013 is expected to positively impact board diversity.

in companies in India. According to a KPMG study conducted in August 2013 on 200 companies (BSE top 200 on the basis of market capitalization), 46.5% companies did not have any women representation on their boards, and only 7% of the board seats were held by women.

Various studies have shown that performance improvement at companies has been enhanced with the addition of women on corporate boards. So what holds women back from reaching the top? And what needs to be done to increase the representation of women at the top rungs of the corporate ladder?

Companies need to graduate from mere compliance and drive change that is foundational – the overall ethos of an organisation's environment must facilitate equal opportunity. Increased budgets need to be reserved for the training and development of women to induct them on boards. Perceptions across India Inc. need to evolve to view women professionals as catalysts of positive change through diversity. Companies must work towards the closure of the gender divide, as well as the deficit that women face in visibility and networking opportunities at the workplace.

The most important and far-reaching change needed is that of perception or mindset of CEOs, board directors, and manager – which are currently dominated by males – working towards the acceptance of women in top management and decision-making positions. Progression in mentality towards enhanced diversity in corporate leadership can effect long-term change. The need of the hour is to reinvent organisational ecosystems to foster equal opportunities enterprise-wide.

The real test is to develop the foresight and maturity to reflect diversity in the Indian boardroom – where women, just like their male counterparts, serve as key components in the wheels of change – towards diversity for a forward-thinking, innovative and productive leadership

BUILDING SENSITIVE, SUSTAINABLE, AND SENSIBLE ORGANISATIONS
Reverse Mentoring of Male Managers

12

The most important question for corporate India today is:
   Who will mentor the men in the workplace?

Let us never forget that: on the eve of India's 65th Republic Day, India was reeling from a violent assault on a young woman professional, Nirbhaya, on the streets of New Delhi, that shook the conscience of the entire nation and the people of this country. In his 65th Republic Day Speech to the nation, the President of India Pranab Mukhejee, cautioned the nation:

'The sanctity of a woman is a directive principle of that larger edifice called Indian civilisation. The Vedas say that there is more than one kind of mother: birth mother, a guru's wife, a king's wife, a priest's wife, she who nurses us, and our motherland. Mother is our protection from evil and oppression, our symbol of life and prosperity. When we brutalise a woman, we wound the soul of our civilisation.

It is time for the nation to reset its moral compass. Nothing should be allowed to spur cynicism, as cynicism is blind to morality. We must look deep into our conscience and find out where we have faltered. The solutions to problems have to be found through discussion and conciliation of views. People must believe that *governance is an instrument for good and for that, we must ensure good governance.'*

And yet this violent "mindset" – continuous to ravage the streets of India – from the cities of Uttar Pradesh, to the homes of young women brides, to the corporate hallways of gender-discrimination. And not enough voices are heard about building gender-sensitivity among male managers and male senior leadership – as if the entire mentoring needs to be for the women alone.

There are endless "initiatives" launched by groups of male senior leaders from Tata Group, American Express India, Microsoft India, PepsiCo India, Deloitte, National HRD Networks, and almost every company – for mentoring women. The reality is that the men themselves first need to mentor their own mind-sets on exactly what the women want in the workplace – and what the women need to be mentored in, and how to provide equal opportunity to women, without making the women feel that they are the "lesser species in the workplace".

At the Informal WILL Tea Meeting with women professionals – we asked *what **exactly do the men in the workplace need mentoring on.*** Following is a slice of what we heard – from the troubled successor-generation of women of corporate India:

22 Most common Gender-biases which men need to discard

WILL Forum Survey: 2014

- Women always need to leave the office at closing time: i.e. 5:00 p.m.
- Women are not open to extended working hours, including weekends, if required.
- Women who do "after-office work" are perceived as compromising on their family responsibilities.

- Women will leave their jobs once they get married.
- Women tend to request more "care-leave" for their parents, in-laws/children/sick leaves.
- Women are not seen as the "primary income earners" of their family.
- Women are not serious about their careers and the efforts invested by the manager/company may be wasted.
- Companies are already providing sufficient benefits and support to women employees, e.g. maternity leave is still considered a "benefit" in some organisations!
- Extended career plans are not discussed with women, as it is perceived that they may not return to work after maternity and just decide to stay at home.
- Women are not strong enough, and do not have the strength/ stamina to work long hours.
- Women are not open to being mobile for international assignments due to family constraint –including single women.
- Women will not hesitate to leave their jobs to follow their spouses, if they get transferred or move to other cities.
- Women do not have the emotional resilience to handle high stress jobs, with high negotiation, and strategic thinking.
- Women lack confidence, to get the job done and get to the front-line.
- Women who demonstrate capabilities at work and make tough decisions are considered to "act like men" and counter- labeled as "aggressive" and "bossy".
- Accomplished men are seen as positive go-getters – while competitive and accomplished women are seen negatively, as aggressive.
- Women leaders who are collaborative and rely on teamwork, rather than command-and-control, are considered to be weak.
- Successful women may have comprised their values or made

adjustments to reach their positions, as they are not perceived as naturally good strong leaders.

- Women are not good in technical, financial, or commercial roles, and are better suited for support and softer functions – like HR, communications, CSR.
- There are not enough talented women who aspire to grow into senior levels.
- Men generally *perceive* an "aspiration-deficit" among women.
- Women need to qualify for top corporate positions and board director roles, while this is never applied to the male candidates.

Although all these biases may seem simplistic – or repetitive and clichéd – the reality is that these perceptions and conscious biases are the root of the socio-economic conditioning of the male mindset in India, and need a structured mentoring program to disperse these biases.

Reverse Mentoring of Male Managers: Preparing for Cultural Transition

Meet Matangi Gowrishankar, Global Head of Capability Development, BP.

Matangi is part of the "substantive women" who have given plenty of time to understanding cultural transition in large organisations, and has been a front-runner at the mission for women in leadership in India. Her work on "reverse mentoring" at the WILL Forum is a pre-courser to how the "new normal in the workplace" will look like – and how generations of men and women need to "unlearn" so many traditional insights – before they can embrace diversity in its true form.

While we cannot begin to change the social fabric and the cultural basis of "gender", if we are to create a level playing field at the workplace, it is imperative that we support organisations to believe that we can practically unlearn conventional approaches and create a "unisex" approach to leadership and working.

Interestingly, as the armed forces, paramilitary forces and the police force begin to be more gender inclusive – there does not seem to be the same concern around distinctive styles of men and women leaders. The expectation of leadership is that we get the job done, we motivate and inspire our teams to achieve extraordinary results and uphold the honour and privilege of being a member of these forces. Why then should there be a dilemma in the Corporate hallways?

One way of dealing with this dilemma is Reverse Mentoring. While reverse mentoring is commonly associated with dealing with issues related to generations at work, we believe that the time has come for reverse mentoring to support the "deconstruction" of gender in the workplace.

The best way to lead sustainable change is to ensure that we influence each successive level within the organisation. It is also about **creating a mindset of a level playing field** – and not just through supporting eco systems.

So, what are the big mindset shifts we need to achieve in this process?

Mindsets of the current leadership icons – majority of whom are presently male – **need to think like the following:**
- My way to the top is not an entitlement – it is something to be achieved
- *I can be successful in my career* **ONLY** *if I meet the needs and aspirations of the diverse people I work with*
- *People I work with also have aspirations and have an* **equal chance at succeeding,** *as I do – so* **collaboration is key**
- I need to stay contemporary in thought and action to proactively manage my success

These mindset shifts cannot be achieved only through training programs, HR practices and systems and the CEO espousing a vision. It needs to happen at the grassroots, and in a non-threatening manner where the focus is on collaboration, learning together and freeing the mind of self-limiting traditions and biases.

Some best practices that can be used for building as part of a "reverse mentoring" program will be the following:
- For all management trainees or new entrants – where *buddy programs* exist – buddies should be of the opposite gender.
- Buddies should be trained to speak in gender neutral terms and support the new entrant to really understand the values of the company and the foundation for success.
- There should be regular open sessions where there is reverse role playing of how a business issue or team issue is resolved.
- Buddies should help each other understand the impact of their behaviours on the motivation and self-esteem of team members. They should have an open conversation around the intended and unintended consequences of behaviours and approaches – and how they might attempt a different behaviour.
- There should be structured "Mentoring" programs for male managers, on the importance of diversity, women in leadership, and balanced boards in the workplace, to stay on the competitive edge of innovation.

I am constantly surprised at how un-abashedly the companies tell us that they have 150 male managers who are currently mentoring women in the organisation, at all levels!

Or large forum that applaud themselves on "Male Champions" who will mentor the women.

My question to them is – how do we know that the 150 men have the right mind-set themselves for mentoring women?

*Who is benchmarking the **appropriate-ness** of the male mentors and sponsors?*

Or are they mentors and sponsors – only because they have achieved a good business performance? Business performance alone – however does not qualify any male manager or leader to mentor any women.

The tragedy of the business format has been that Business Performance alone has led the way for leadership assessment – without any reflection on sustainability, social communities, environment, equality of people – which have all been "squashed" in the workplace, at the altar of market capitalisation and quarterly revenue generation statements from CEOs.

So, we come back to the question of: Who will Mentor the Men?

And, it is time that all the companies embraced this important "bend in the curve" – and stop using clichés like "unlearn" or "reinvent" –

It is clearly to be stated as *"**Gender-Sensitive Leadership Program" for male managers.***

According to Matangi Gowrishankar of BP:

'Interesting, when we look around companies – the so-called "Mentors and Sponsors" are largely chosen from amongst successful men – both for men and women high potential talent. This only serves to perpetuate a "male" definition of success and leadership. Companies that seek to make a real difference should ensure that high potential male talent be mentored by the successful women role models in the organisation. This will help to keep the conversations going and enable men to think about alternative routes to success and to understand that as we reach the top – a more gender neutral approach to leadership is what really works.'

While a majority of men in positions of influence and decision making today might be of a generation that accepted the male gender construct – it would seem that the newer generations are increasingly flouting this. A male mentoring program in the corporate world that *supports the men to be strong and responsible leaders of* tomorrow can provide a valuable platform for them to explore areas such as behavior, values, confidence, academics, teamwork, self-esteem, conflict resolution, healthy relationship building. *The focus is really to build successful, wise and gifted members of society and the workplace – people who are comfortable about leading the change.*

This is where all the women of India have a high responsibility in mentoring their sons – to become wise, responsible, and gifted members of society.

Building Gender Sensitive Leadership
Structuring a reverse-mentoring program for male managers

Year 2010

Meet Raj Raghavan, Director HR, Amazon India

One of the few real-time leaders of Balanced Leadership – who I met in the early years when we started the WILL Forum India – and who was then leading HR at GE India, Jack Welch Technology Center at Bangalore. There is something about Raj Raghavan that endears people to his accomplishment, style of delivery, open mind-set, and very global cultural sensitivity – including that of women and how the companies can embrace the value of women for diversity and innovation. As early as 2010 – Raj Raghavan presented a most excellent roadmap on mentoring male managers to the group of women and men who had gathered at the Microsoft office campus in Hyderabad – for the WILL Forum meeting.

According to Raj Raghavan – *The "Purpose"* of any sensible mentoring program for male managers, would have the following agenda:

- Inculcating "Balanced Leadership" principles and practice across corporations
- To facilitate and leverage leaders as champions and mentors of balanced leadership
- Build Accountability to challenge and sustain this change

While setting the Context for a successful male mentoring program – companies will need to understand how to "Build Awareness and Fairness" in a conservative workplace, where:

- "Balanced Leadership" is not very well known or understood well; diversity in leadership is often considered "nice" to do rather than business reality
- Very few men leaders have had a female mentor in their career
- Most leaders possess a reasonable/ strong sense of fair play (i.e. a generalised concern about inequity in society) but do not know how to go about getting it to work

The *content of* such a program should focus on:

- How to support Men in order to support Women/Men
- How to Create Paradigm change/ mindset shift
- How to inculcate the concept of RESPECT for the other gender (Sensitivity to gender + Value + Meritocracy)
- How to help men understand Women/Capability /Competency
- Help men with how to work on collaborative techniques
- Work on spreading the concept of diversity for innovation, business growth and the competitive edge
  Why then do we have so few mentoring programs for male

managers on gender-sensitive leadership in corporate India – and why do the men perceive it almost an embarrassment to attend such programs? Clearly, male leaders in corporate India have a fear of losing status – or of being seen as part of the problem. There is an additional sense of Apathy – a sense that issues of gender do not concern men. There is unfortunately also a perception among several women CEOs and business leaders – who believe that the gender-issues are too low a priority to concern them directly. There is further Ignorance – whether perceived or real on the issues concerning women in the workplace. And, finally – Cultural / Societal mindset of men refuses to change.

Even if the Gender-sensitive leadership programs are being conducted – the HR Head, or CFO, or Business Unit heads do not attend these programs – as if the problems belong only to the "lower or mid-level" managers in the organisation.

Until the feudal mindset of HR Leaders and CEOs who plan these programs for their employees – themselves undertake the program, or benchmark their speeches with their real-time actions – they will not be taking any responsibility for the outcome.

I will be unable to leave this chapter – without putting on record the continuing and non-stop "push-back" we have received and continue to receive from the so called "gate-keepers" of the CEOs office, and HR Leaders of several Indian companies– on engaging with the women in leadership programs. Women in these companies continue to write to us – about their "glass ceiling", "sexual harassment issues", and the fact that all is done only as an intervention "on paper" – with no real intent to promote women. The worst case I have heard is of women who are embarrassed about the way "International Women's Day" is celebrated in their organisations – with "goodies" for the women and "photo-ops" for the men. If only the men would ask the women how they would like the International Women's Day to be celebrated –!

SOUL-SISTERS
You will find them Everywhere!

13

My first brush with the courageous and strong women who live in the interior villages of rural India, which is about 60% of the Indian population, was when I went to do famine-relief in drought hit state of Rajasthan, during my college days as a volunteer with the National Social Service (NSS cadets). The women in rural India are a real-time "power-house" – raising families, working in the fields with bare hands, drawing water from the nearest public wells, cooking family meals on dry branches, milking the neighbourhood cows/goats, and dressed in the traditional brightest of colors of red, yellow, and green. I entered their homes with full respect, shared their meals of barley and red chilies, asked them questions about their lives – and understood that they were fiercely conservative, courageous, and protective about their families, their villages, and their traditions. But they were also inquisitive, curious, and dispassionate when they spoke about the politicians, government, and officers who make the rules in their rural areas – and equally distraught that they had no "voice" in the affairs of their districts and law and order. I could see that they were harbouring a secret longing for being more open, articulate and a chance for more opportunity – in whatever way they perceived it.

In the early 1990's – I had the chance to go into the underground open-pit zinc mines of Hindustan Zinc in Udaipur, about 70 meters deep – with my helmet and torch, accompanying the mines officer and my American Embassy colleagues – and experienced how the narrow shaft and dark tunnels, with barely enough oxygen, looked to the toiling coal-miners. When I asked the women in the community if they had gone into the mines – they looked at me with "awe" as if this was not a question to be asked, as it had never occurred to them to do so, and they had no reason to go there anyway.

Then when I was writing the "South Asian Free Trade Area" (SAFTA) as Special Consultant to the SAARC Chamber of Commerce & Industry, in early 2001, I met hundreds of smart and articulate women professionals of Bangladesh, Nepal, and Sri Lanka – who are often seen only in the Chambers of Commerce, when there is a seminar on "women entrepreneurs". The other business meetings are attended only by men of large private limited companies, mainly traders of finance, commodities, and technology based goods – while the women busy themselves in making the famous "Dhaka saree" and bamboo handicraft of the economy – sometime with finance from banks, and at other times from their spouses or homes. I have spent several hours with these women entrepreneurs in South Asia and tried hard to have a conversation on how to find ways to engage them with the mainstream business forums. Their answers always left me admitting that they will not be able to win this battle for equal presence at the male-dominated industry forums, given the sharp politics, and total disregard for the intellectual capacity of women to understand "strategic, geopolitical, or public policy" of the nation.

Similar is my experience with the charming and lovely women of Lahore and Islamabad. How wonderful it was to be invited to the homes of these Pakistani women – how wonderful to share their aristocratic meals – and how wonderful to admire their fashion sense and demeanor. I was also most excited to deliver a lecture to the very bright students at the 100-acre green campus of the Lahore University of Management (LUMS) – and discuss the conflict resolution areas for track-II cooperation in the South Asia region. But how lost for words they all seemed when I asked the women of Lahore and Islamabad, what they think about the politics of democracy, the need for more women in government, the need for more rights for women for gender-parity.

I have lead several Roundtables for women in leadership with the women professionals in city of Lucknow – the conservative city capital of the state of UP in India. The city of Lucknow alone has a population of 2.5 million, roughly equal to the state of Georgia or state of Louisiana in the USA – mainly Shia-Muslim dominated. I have heard the voices of women scientists working on cancer research at the local Institutes, and Principals of local colleges, and established women lawyers, and women journalists in the region. *There is so much hope in their aspirations – and so much despair in their stories.* The college lady principal spoke about how her college was proudly awarded for its work in education, and how the administration requested her "husband" to collect the award "on her behalf" on stage. The cancer research scientist woman spoke about how she never got the opportunity to be nominated for advanced management and research programs, funded by the university, as they were all already cornered by the men

I have watched these "soul sisters" from near – and from afar.

And they are the same – across countries, across geographies, across functions, across homes.

They know what to do – they know what they need – they know how to do it.

But they are all completely helpless in the society, community, and business environment – that has made these women into mid-level mediocre workers – as the dominant species in a biosphere would enslave its other co-habitants, in an unequal world.

The classical verse of Nobel Laureate Guru Rabindra Nath Tagore, Bengali poet and author– still ring so true for the women of India – even after 67 year of independence, after Tagore wrote this verse in 1947:

"Where the mind is without fear and the head is held high
Where knowledge is free
Where the world has not been broken up into fragments
By narrow domestic walls
Where words come out from the depth of truth
Where tireless striving stretches its arms towards perfection
Where the clear stream of reason has not lost its way
Into the dreary desert sand of dead habit
Where the mind is led forward by thee
Into ever-widening thought and action
Into that heaven of freedom, my Father, let my country awake."

TALKING A WALK DOWN MUMBAI'S "RED-LIGHT" AREA

14

Reminiscing high-impact Learnings
   Women doing business of "another kind" and leaving the heart-ache to the health-volunteers
   Obscene corporate salaries – and women sex workers

For those who have never been to the Mumbai "red light area" – and those who would studiously pretend that it does not even exist – let there be enough realism to recognise that in the thriving, profit-making, best – business practice financial capital of India, there are many women who are doing business in another and more soulful way.

I have walked down the Falkand Road in Mumbai, with a group of six other women – all senior editors from leading foreign media and magazines – completely enwrapped with the thought of what I might see. The street had a semi-anglicised name – for reasons completely unknown – but clearly a remnant from the colonial British days of India Raj.

We were led by our escort who was an active aids-health care volunteer, running a private NGO clinic in this area, and who clearly knew his way around well and names of all the ladies who hung out from quarters on this busy street. The entrance to their "homes" was a canal of squalor, where it was difficult to set foot without dirtying your shoes with unknown smelly substances. This was followed by a few stairs until we came to a brightly lit blue door. The cement on the door walls was heavily chipped, and the paint was peeling off the old home-door.

Inside the musty room, three women between the age of 20–45 years were going about their daily household chores. For them, it was just another day to clean up their beds and kitchen – and prepare themselves for the work that will begin again with the clients at night. The older woman was busy washing the dishes with mud-and-ash, while the other two young women were open, friendly, and began to tell us their story.

The beds we were sitting on – were the same beds being used for client-sex. The mattresses were old and torn, the cots were made of jute and wood and a light linen cloth was hung to separate the two cots – so that they could be used at the same time.

The two sex-worker women were at ease with the work they are doing. They earned about Rs. 200 per day (USD 4 only) when income was good – and for this this they needed to solicit business all night long. Their customers were from lower-income groups of Mumbai, and they were all fully exposed to the hazards of HIV and other life-threatening ailments.

The women had no knowledge of the business, finance, and profits of corporate India – or the obscene salaries that CEOs and business leaders in corporate India get paid – for increasing the GDP of the Indian economy and distributing dividends to their shareholders.

Are not the women of the red-light district co-owners of the resources, water, air, sunlight – that business uses for its own private ends?

Is their business so different that they are not even recognised as stakeholders of a judicious economy?

What kind of leadership should these women be defining – and who is going to mentor them to rise above their livelihoods, which has not been the first-choice of their profession?

What kind of a planet will they bequeath to their children?
  Is it not the same planet that you and I live in?

ANNEXURES

WILL MOTHER'S HANDBOOK
Best Practices For New and Entrant Mothers in the Workplace

Fixing the Leaking Leadership Pipeline in Corporate India
Responding to "On-Ramping and Off-Ramping for Women"

- Introduction to the Leadership pipeline
- Women in leadership roles – Gender Gap
- Off Ramp and On Ramp – Decisions made by women
- Why is the Leadership pipeline leaking?
- Focus areas for organizations
- Fixing the leakage

* *

At the entry level men and women are hired in the same ratio… Evidence exists that women are lost through the pipeline by voluntary termination at least three times faster than men once they reach mid level management.

* *

Leadership Pipeline

This analogy of a pipeline in relation to leaders is very effective. The importance of creating a pool of talented individuals who will take the organisation forward is critical.

＊＊＊＊＊＊＊＊＊＊＊＊＊＊＊＊＊＊＊＊＊＊＊＊

- Demand for leaders is high – only 35 percent women are employed as against 85 percent men
- Natural leaders are as rare as natural athletes
- Leaders are developed over time – investment in them is a long process

Women in Leadership Roles

FIGURE 12:
LEADERSHIP GENDER GAP IN INDIA INC.

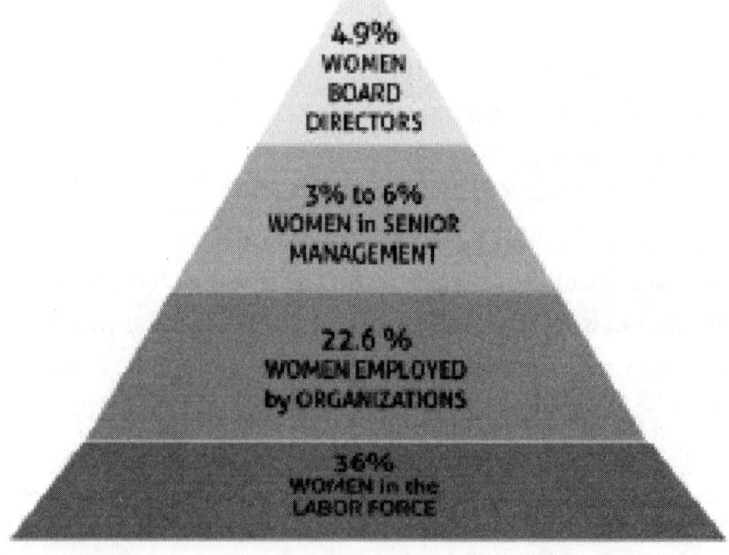

4.9%
WOMEN
BOARD
DIRECTORS

3% to 6%
WOMEN in SENIOR
MANAGEMENT

22.6 %
WOMEN EMPLOYED
by ORGANIZATIONS

36%
WOMEN in the
LABOR FORCE

Off-Ramp and On-Ramp decisions made by Women

FIGURE 13:

Decisions taken by women
<u>Reality is...</u>

FIGURE 14:

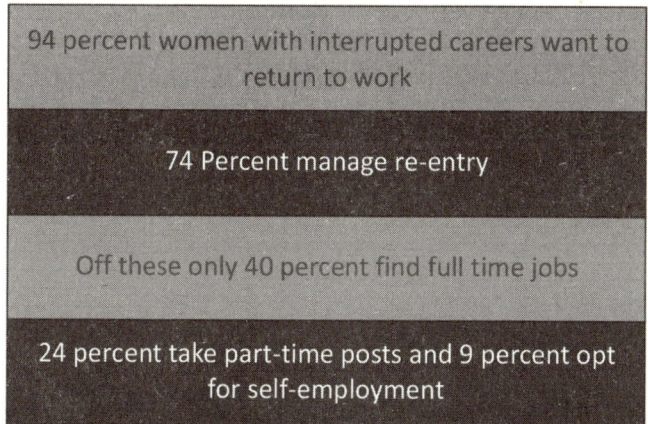

Therefore, the reasons for leakage are...

The double bind

- Extreme perceptions – Too soft, too tough and never just right
- Competent but disliked – women leaders are perceived as competent or likable, rarely both – 32 percent men called attention to this predicament over 25 percent women

Glass ceiling or the labyrinth

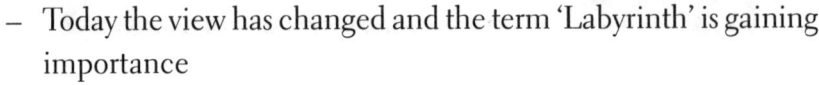

- In the 1970s women started entering the workforce
- Women encountered societal and organisational constraints – these obstructions were termed
- The Glass Ceiling
- Today the view has changed and the term 'Labyrinth' is gaining importance

Common issues raised

- Opportunities – Known or communicated
- Perceived lack of skills and experience
- Career path clarity
- Lack of role models
- Focus on external exposure than internal

To fix the gap...organisations need to understand...

Similar values and goals

Men and women have similar work values and goals –
- Challenging job
- Supportive workplace

- Strong values
- A good fit between life on and off the job
- Opportunities for high achievement
- Good compensation

Statistics – Similar values and goals

FIGURE 15:

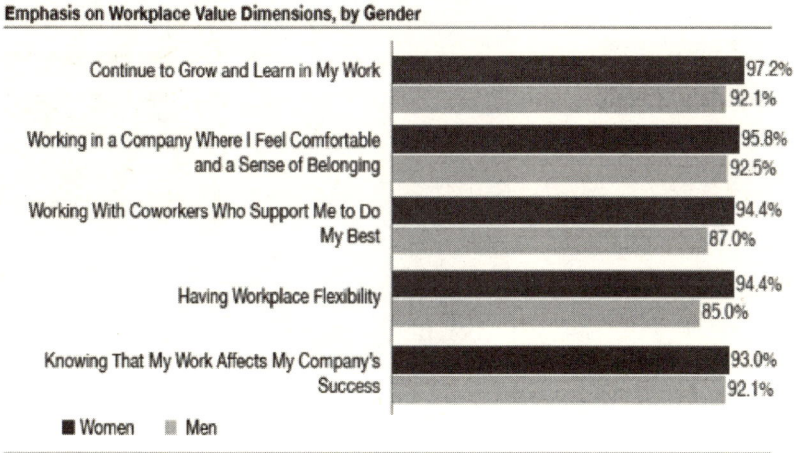

Emphasis on Workplace Value Dimensions, by Gender

Continue to Grow and Learn in My Work — 97.2% / 92.1%

Working in a Company Where I Feel Comfortable and a Sense of Belonging — 95.8% / 92.5%

Working With Coworkers Who Support Me to Do My Best — 94.4% / 87.0%

Having Workplace Flexibility — 94.4% / 85.0%

Knowing That My Work Affects My Company's Success — 93.0% / 92.1%

■ Women   ■ Men

Common ground
- **Decision Making Opportunities available –**
  - Access to resources
  - Work opportunities – 43 percent people agree on similar work opportunities
  - Sound Management Acumen – Communicate and adapt to culture –
  - Managing teams
  - Managing work and clients

There are common leadership traits…some that men excel at and some where women do better

Leadership Attributes – Men and Women

FIGURE 16:

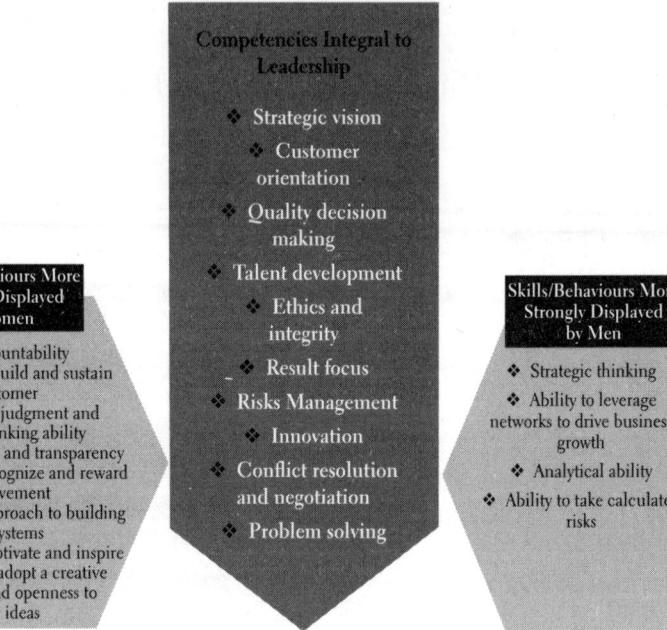

Competencies Integral to Leadership

❖ Strategic vision
❖ Customer orientation
❖ Quality decision making
❖ Talent development
❖ Ethics and integrity
❖ Result focus
❖ Risks Management
❖ Innovation
❖ Conflict resolution and negotiation
❖ Problem solving

Skills/Behaviours More Strongly Displayed by Women

❖ Accountability
❖ Ability to build and sustain customer
❖ Intuitive judgment and critical thinking ability
❖ Compliance and transparency
❖ Ability to recognize and reward achievement
❖ Inclusive approach to building ecosystems
❖ Ability to motivate and inspire
❖ Ability to adopt a creative approach and openness to new ideas

Skills/Behaviours More Strongly Displayed by Men

❖ Strategic thinking
❖ Ability to leverage networks to drive business growth
❖ Analytical ability
❖ Ability to take calculated risks

Key attributes – Women

- **Women as effective crisis management leaders –**
  - Consistent and rational in making decisions
  - Risk averse
  - Conservative over money matters
- **Women and ethical leadership –**
  - Inculcating and propagating values
  - Adept at setting and defining values for self and the workplace

Activity
What should organisations do to fix the gap?

The true test of an organisation's skill at creating effective leaders... lies in the organisation's ability to consistently and systematically develops strong managers at every level."

– Jack Welch

Workplace Ethos for promoting Leadership

- Balanced leadership – promote diversity and inclusion
- Focused career progression planning
- Talent Management strategies
- Define performance standards at each level

Workplace Ethos for promoting Leadership

- Special Leadership training
- Access to corporate networking groups
- Opportunities for higher-level progress (Overseas posting or secondment)

Promoting leadership for individuals

1. Ambition is given option – Career Arc flexibility
2. On ramp opportunities created
3. Face time demands reduced
4. Personal motivational lifestyles appreciated
5. Life skills development encouraged

Leadership is not gender-specific
It is nurtured with experience, mentoring, and releasing the "power of self"
Leadership is an experience, and there must be equal opportunity for all segments to experience leadership in business and society

****

50 Mother's Most Popular Practices in Corporate India

Wᴵᴸᴸ

Mother's
Handbook
****

Career and Performance Related Practices For New and
Expectant Mother's

1. Fully paid maternity leave. This leave could be for 12-weeks or more, depending on the prevailing local regulations or company best practice policies.

2. Performance rating for new and entrant mothers will not be affected by their absence from work during maternity.
   - *If maternity has been availed, post mid-year, then the mid-year rating will hold good, unless a strong case is presented for a downgrade during ATR's*
   - *Low performance rating can be awarded only if there's ample documented evidence of non-performance*
   - *Women returning from maternity leave post mid-year can be treated similar to a new joiner since he/she hasn't had a scope for showing performance (this implies an average rating performance).*

3. Active support from the team manager or business leaders, to organize the workload of expectant mothers going on maternity leave, while ensuring continued performance of the team in their absence

4. Performance appraisal guidelines from CEO and HR must clearly communicate that maternity, long leave and special leaves are given appropriate ratings, and should be

W<small>ILL</small>

transparently communicated and implemented across the organization.

5. "On-ramping" of women employees who return from maternity – Re skilling and Re-integrating as a key priority to engage them back to work

6. Flexi-time work policies for new and entrant mothers, during for the first year of their return from maternity.

   This can be equally applied by manufacturing, finance, banking, IT-related, pharma. Hospitality, telecommunications – and all sectors of the economy. Flexi-time policies for new and entrant mothers – are not sector or industry specific.

7. Options to Work from home during maternity – especially if this is part of the medical advise to expectant mothers.

8. Engage or Assigning a mentor/ "buddy" to the new mother's when they come back – preferably, a lady who has come back from Maternity Leave in the last 1 year and has got back into normal office work

9. Mass career customization' for women who return from maternity – dial-up and dial-down of work timings and performance measures

WILL

10. Gender sensitization and awareness training programs for other employees and managers, on the guidelines on how to work with new and entrant mothers and create a nurturing environment for them

11. Specific "Work Initiatives" for mothers resuming back to work, which can be done through the organizations Women's and Diversity Networks

12. Grievance Redressal Council – especially for women employees who have resumed post maternity

13. Reorientation Programme:
    - For bringing the employees on LWP/Maternity Leave up to speed regarding the Changes/Updates in various policy and process (if any)
    - Creating a conducive work environment to help the associate ease back into their work-related responsibilities more efficiently.
    - Aiding through a structured program, the re-orientation of such associates

14. Special Performance Management Policy for the women returning from Maternity Leave.
    This policy ensures women who are returning from Maternity

Leave or Childcare leave, would have their final performance band calculated based on all available Performance Ratings during the year.

15. The leave without pay policy and a progressive childcare policy can be extended for employees, which enables them to avail of leaves when it's required the most.

Nurturing and Well being practices

16. Congratulatory Triggers are sent to those who have applied for maternity and Paternity leave. This practice is usually very well received and has tremendous emotive appeal.

17. Full time Day care Centers—as on campus or as link-ups with external day care centers

18. Creating a maternity resting room for pregnant women and new mothers, on the company premises

19. Healthy food counters, healthy nutrients available on special menus from cafeteria – for expectant mothers.

20. A "Stay Connected Program" for women on maternity leave via email and intra-company online programs – to *ensure that associates on long leave continue to be updated with the latest happenings, receive news, and information bytes – in the comfort of their personal email boxes on a monthly basis that help them keep updated*

21. "Workplace Parents Group" should be formed across various centers to engage working parents through child psychology and parenting workshops. *These groups bring*

WILL

working parents together to discuss common problems and look for solutions.

22. **Extendable Maternity Leave** – *Maternity Leave (paid) is for 12 weeks. A woman suffering from illness arising out of pregnancy, delivery, or premature birth of child, miscarriage, medical termination of pregnancy or tubectomy is entitled to an additional paid leave for a maximum period of one month upon providing the required supporting medical documents*

23. **Special transport allowance for expecting mothers-vehicle drop to their residence escorted by armed security guard.**

24. **In house 24 * 7 gymnasium and doctors on campus**

25. **Crèche on campus**

26. **TOS (Time off Scheme) to encourage work life balance is in place.**

27. **During prenatal, post natal and finally resuming back**
    - **No docking of compensation is done.**
    - **Maternity or paternity leave does not affect associate's eligibility for ESOP**

28. **Exception handling in terms of transport, dress code.**

29. **Health advisory committee to who gives health tips.**

30. **Maternity treatment at cashless hospitals.**

31. **Domiciliary and consulting services available on campus**

32. **Complaint mechanism for redressal of grievances.**

33. **Congratulations-maternity leave benefit**

34. **Return to work Policy for New Mothers:** *Women can decide their date of return to work as per the doctors advise*

W<small>ILL</small>

and discussion with their HR Managers. Their employment status with the company is not affected in any way by their maternity leave.

35. Special Car parking reservation for new and experience mother's

36. Mother's resting and feeding room

37. Personal felicitations for new mothers returning to Work!

38. On site rejuvenation lounge – for new and entrant mothers

39. Maternity Coaching is an opportunity

40. All female employees who are returning from maternity leave get an option to work at a reduced schedule of 50% of the normal weekly hours per week, for a 2 month transition period immediately following the maternity leave

41. Job sharing between two women – as an option for reducing the work-load for new mothers

42. Voluntary reduced work hours after motherhood

43. Part Time Employment – *Employees reduce their workload and consequently their hours decrease to fewer than standard workweek requirements. Part-time employees work between 20–30 hours per week with a corresponding reduction in pay and adjustment of benefits.*

44. Sabbatical Leave – as an extension of maternity leave

45. Transfers/Re-location made easy for spouses and married women

46. Promote Internal Networking Platforms for women – where they can chat, and share their experiences, and challenges

Will

47. **Concierge Services** – in India and globally during travel for work and business meetings

48. **Ombudsperson Policy**: *employees can raise an integrity concern to the Ombuds person through various channels and immediate investigation is done and appropriate action is taken. An employee can also raise a concern anonymously by dropping a note at the Ombuds boxes placed across locations*

49. **24hr convenience store** – *tied up with grocery stores where the employees can place all their grocery orders online and the orders will be delivered to them in office each Friday. This helps them focus on work and personal life and leave the other odds to tie up in office*

50. **Provide light-weight laptops and cell phone to new mothers** – so that they are easy to carry to work

ASSESSING THE RETURN ON INVESTMENT IN WOMEN
Quantifying the Balanced Leadership Value

When faced with the proposal for "Balanced Leadership," companies continue to ask the question: 'What is the economic value that gender-diversity brings to the business and to corporate boardrooms?'

However, not everything that is valuable is quantifiable, and quantification of intangibles carries a large degree of academic risk. There could be more than one definition of the value domain, and there could be more than one way of mapping each domain variable to a value function (i.e. to a particular value from a range of strategic values.) This is not therefore a task that would be taken up lightly by businesses and economists. However, given the insistence of CEOs, corporate boards, and senior company leaders on the need for placing a value or correlation on "women and wealth-creation" – it is time to provide a realistic tool that will reveal the domains of value that are unlocked by gender-balance at leadership levels in companies, and it remains an important endeavour to delineate such a tool.

Framing the Question of Value and Enterprise Risk

At the outset, it is important to correctly formulate the question being studied. Lack of clarity, or confusion over the research question has been the first serious constraint in dealing with this issue. The objective should not be aimed at making conclusive statements about the differentiated effectiveness of women in performing certain business roles – for example whether they are intrinsically better sales persons for educational products, or better scientists, or better chefs. While traditionally, certain roles have been gender-stereotyped because of the dominant presence of either gender in those roles (such as teaching, nursing, etc.) the earlier WILL-KPMG reports have shown no conclusive evidence that either gender is predominantly superior in performing any particular roles, nor is it our purpose to make any assertion in this regard.*

Performance in a role is conditioned by many externalities. It would therefore not be correct to state that women perform better than men in certain roles, and that is not the purpose of this study. Our efforts are aimed towards formulating an approach that will help CEO's and corporate boards to better understand the sources of value that are unlocked by "Balanced Leadership."

a.The contributions of the values of diversity and inclusion (D&I) in a globalised business environment have been widely studied, debated and documented. Chief among the contributions of a D&I culture to the business organization is 'enterprise risk-management'. Risk is measured as the probability of occurrence multiplied by the value exposed. Not surprisingly, "risk" is very hard to quantify, and the probability of occurrence of a "risk-event" remains a subjective estimate. Very often, low-likelihood events are completely ruled out or overlooked by the team of financial and legal experts that constitute the present traditional-style corporate boardrooms.**

* *Refer: WILL-KPMG Report "Differentiating Styles of Women in Leadership", WILL Forum India, 2010*
** *Refer: WILL-KPMG Report "Women and Enterprise Risk Management" WILL Forum India, 2011*

However, as has been widely discussed in recent times and especially in the context of the financial debacles of 2008–09 – "high-risk, low-likelihood" events seem to be occurring more often than ever before, due to the fast-changing dynamics of the business and external environment, including technology. The recent crash of Lehman Brothers and the political transition in countries like Egypt, are good examples of highly-impactful global "non-financial risks" which was not part of the corporate risk-dashboard in the best companies worldwide.

Thus, distribution models of "risk" – as a factor for business forecast – are being challenged and re-evaluated. And, therefore one of the vital indicators of the economic value of "balanced leadership" poses signficant quantification challenges – at the very outset.

b. There are other constraints to a study of this nature. "Business Value" is contributed by many aspects of a business, including tangible and intangible business assets. The leadership attributes leveraged by a company are based on the company's value system. Often the value system is poorly understood within the company, often poorly articulated by the leadership and itself poorly valued! Secondly, personal attributes are leveraged differently in different business activities and what may be an advantage in a particular role may not be so in another. For example, one of the gender-specific attributes that has been widely documented is 'empathy'. This attribute has many and varied economic manifestations in the business context – including customer satisfaction, product development, stakeholder management, team building, etc. All of these are important aspects of the business delivery process. However, the value so created is spatially distributed across a range of business verticals and line-roles, and is hard to capture in one single measure.

The above discussion underlines the dimensions of the constraints in determining or assigning an exact economic value contributed by a balanced workforce, and balanced leadership –

which is probably why it has so far not been measured in economic terms by companies.

The WILL Balanced Leaderhip Value Model

Quantifying the Economic Value of Women to Business

The purpose of this exposition is to set out a possible approach towards quantifying the economic value created by leveraging gender-diversity in the enterprise and particularly at leadership levels.

The conceptual model is expressed as a simple and evocative function:

$E = f(\Sigma)$, f being some mathematical function of the sum of several individual values.

This simple articulation represents the objective of quantifying the differential contribution made by women leaders, or balanced leadership, in the business.

The simple mathematical representation will use known gender-specific behaviours at leadership levels and assume that business values could be associated with those behaviours. For example, in the case of 'empathy' as a specific behaviour, we assume that the value of this behaviour in a sales context can be assigned. When several different attributes are being considered at the same time, the economic values associated with each behaviour can be normalised (assign a value of 1 to each) and emphasised by assigning different weightages.

Our simple relationship $E=f(\Sigma)$ thus represents the weighted addition of the values associated with various (i.e., a finite selection of) gender-specific leadership behaviours.

The WILL-KPMG study (2009, New Delhi) on "Creating Women Business Leaders: Differentiating Styles of Women Executives" identified several personality and motivational factors that underlie gender-differentiated styles in leadership. These findings are in line with the findings of other studies reported from across the globe.

Gender-specific attributes characteristic of the leadership style of women included, for example, the following:

1. Inclusive behaviours
2. Transparency
3. Empathy (listening skills)
4. Trust-based relationships (with customers, clients)
5. Balanced decision-making

The above attributes of women leaders potentially deliver accentuated value in the context of specific business activities, such as for example:

1. Strategy & Planning
2. Brand & Reputation
3. Product Development & Operations
4. Sales & Marketing
5. Talent Development
6. Finance

Note that we specifically focus on leadership behaviours. We are talking about leadership behaviours that leverage gender-specific attributes.

We propose that gender-specific attributes offer additional economic value which can be modeled conceptually as the weighted sum of the assumed economic value associated with those attributes. The model thus is:

$$E = \Sigma w_i A_i$$

where wi is the weightage associated with the specific attributed Ai.

Acknowledging that the weights are dependent upon the business context, we may further specify the model as follows:-

$$E_c = \Sigma w_{ic} A_{ic}$$

Thus we have a conceptual model for how each business context (or role) – designated by the subscript c – leverages the specific value provided by gender-specific attributes.

The above equation can be summarised as:

$$E = W.A$$

- where E is the vector of outcomes, being the differentiated economic value associated with the contribution of women leaders in a set of (m) identified business contexts;
- W is the m x n matrix of weights reflecting the importance of a given gender-specific attribute in a particular business context;
- A is the n x 1 vector of (n) economic values associated with gender-specific attributes that are recognised and valued in business.

It is assumed that there are m business contexts and n gender-specific attributes that are recognised and valued by business enterprises. In the above example, m = 6 and n = 5.

The WILL-KPMG study provides a list of attributes, as earlier mentioned. A list of potential business roles or activities is also listed above. Taking the combination of 5 Attribtutes and 6 Business Contexts, we have 6 equations each with 5 different variables. Assuming the variables are mutually independent (and therefore there is no double-counting of value), these linear equations provide a simple but potentially powerful tool to estimate the economic value generated by women leaders in the organization.

The model delivers the differentiated economic value obtained by leveraging gender-specific leadership behaviours in each of those 6 business contexts.

By cranking up or down the weights and the economic value associations with each attributes (attributes could potentially have negative economic values), a practitioner in need of a tool to assess the specific contribution of leveraging gender diversity and would be able to understand better how diversity at leadership levels affects the profitability of the company.

Embedding the WILL Balanced Leadership Value Formula into the Company Board Decision Making

The purpose of the present exercise is to set out an approach or a methodology by which the CEO question "what is the differentiated economic value contributed by balanced leadership" may be responded to. It is not intended that a specific value should be evaluated in a general sense. It will be up to each business leader to use this model to assess what attributes he/she is seeking and securing in the quest to develop a robust and sustainable business organisation.

The model is purely conceptual and in each case needs to be tailored, detailed out and validated for use.

Questions that CEOs must ask and answer for themselves include:

1. What are the economic values associated with the gender-differentiated leadership attributes? In other words, how would a particular gender-specific attribute, be valued?

2. What weight does a particular attribute deserve in the context of a particular business operation?

3. How well does the model reflect the incremental gender-specific economic values (since there are values associated with the leadership styles of men as well)?

The purpose will not be formulate an answer for each CEO – but only to provide a framework for addressing the question.

CEOs must recognise that gender-specific attributes – on which there is plenty of literature and research – contribute specifically to each of their business operations and situations. CEOs and boards must begin to acknowledge that if these attributes are appropriately weighted, the differential value can be specifically understood. They must also recognise that failing to leverage these attributes takes this opportunity away from the business enterprise, thus destroys a potential source of value.

What corporate India requires is a balanced evaluation based on a balanced distribution of weights across a range of behavioural choices, especially when made by senior executives who are at leadership levels. The balancing of the portfolio of behavioural attributes to account for preferred male and female leadership behaviours – will help to correct the imbalance in executive evaluations that eliminate women from the race to top level positions.

In conclusion, The WILL Balanced Leadership Value Model proposes theat companies:

– Formulate a balanced set of behavioural preferences that achieve the company's goals

– Consciously evaluate what behavioural preferences are really valuable in the context of a particular job role in the company and to formally assign weightages to those behaviours irrespective of gender

– Consciously attribute appropriate weightages across this set, (instead of assigning all the weights to one half and none to the other half

Source: WILL KPMG Report "Women and Wealth Creation: Assessing the Return on Investment in Women"
Credits to:
Dr Shailaja D Sharma, Director SSense Intelligence & Adjunct Faculty, National Institute of Advanced Studies (NIAS)

TESTING THE WATERS: FOR WOMEN ON BOARDS

Is there a lack of qualified women – or is there lack of Opportunity for qualified women?
  WILL KPMG Survey Findings: 2013 – Annexure

They play a pivotal role in the overall professional workforce; yet, they continue to battle inequality of opportunity. For years, women professionals have been denied their dues, especially in terms of adequate representation in the top echelons of the corporate world. Why?

Over several years, this gender-imbalance has been credited to the disinterest among corporate entities in facilitating the growth of women; and to preconceived notions that management across organisations harbour, that women professionals will eventually switch priorities from the workplace to home responsibilities – often referred to the "off-ramping" of women.

Despite the growing career aspirations of women professionals cross the socioeconomic landscape, why are companies so apprehensive to invest in the sustained growth of their women executives?

Chart: Current profile of women executives across companies in corporate India:

FIGURE 17:

Percentage of women employees in the organisation (full-time staff only)

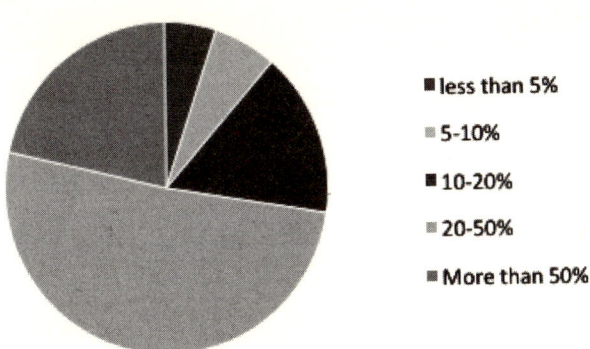

- less than 5%
- 5-10%
- 10-20%
- 20-50%
- More than 50%

Source: WILL-KPMG's survey on balanced boards, 2013

FIGURE 18:

Percentage of women in top management (senior management and CXO level)

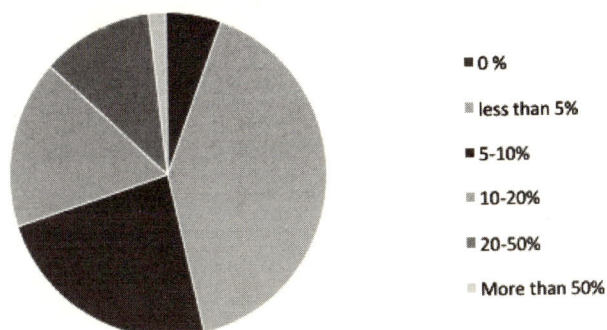

- 0%
- less than 5%
- 5-10%
- 10-20%
- 20-50%
- More than 50%

Source: WILL-KPMG's survey on balanced boards, 2013

To seek possible answers to such questions – and to gauge the root cause of corporate resistance to balanced leadership – the Forum for Women in Leadership (WILL Forum India), in collaboration with KPMG in India, has conducted a survey of India's business leaders and top executives. The survey explores the trends, drivers and challenges related to the concept of balanced boards. It strives to evaluate and highlight the need for companies to value the increased representation of women in senior leadership positions for enhancing business performance through balanced leadership.

TABLE 3:

Methodology and design		
The survey encompasses	Collation of survey responses	
• The need to invest in women professionals • The various constraints associated with nominating women as members of corporate boards • Critical business qualities of corporate leadership that can be introduced or strengthened by increasing women's representation on boards • The impact of increased women's representation on various parameters of business performance • Factors that help women on corporate boards to contribute to good governance • Reasons for poor gender diversity in Indian corporate boards vis-à-vis other countries • How organisations can encourage and support women to assume corporate leadership roles	• Responses mapped under the respective Categories	• All responses calculated in percentages to determine proportions

Respondent profile

The WILL-KPMG 2013 survey reflects the thoughts of 175 leaders – both men and women – who constitute leadership or top management positions in both public and private enterprises, across disciplines and industries – from pharmaceuticals and healthcare, oil and gas and manufacturing to automotive, consulting, financial services and IT/ITES.

Industry sample

FIGURE 19:

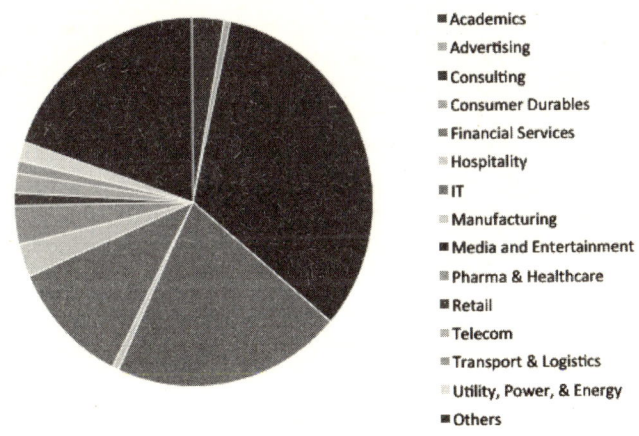

- ■ Academics
- ▨ Advertising
- ■ Consulting
- ▨ Consumer Durables
- ▨ Financial Services
- ▨ Hospitality
- ▨ IT
- ▨ Manufacturing
- ■ Media and Entertainment
- ▨ Pharma & Healthcare
- ■ Retail
- ▨ Telecom
- ▨ Transport & Logistics
- ▨ Utility, Power, & Energy
- ■ Others

Source: WILL-KPMG's survey on balanced boards, 2013

The gender profile of the respondent sample is characterized by 82.2% women and 17.8% men. The educational profiles of the respondents are diverse, with postgraduates accounting for nearly 61% and professional degree or diploma holders constituting almost 19% of the sample.

The private sector's strong influence on India is evident, with more than 87% of the respondents representing this sector, particularly in the IT, consulting and financial services verticals. The respondents are represented from across designations and levels, ranging from C-level leaders to senior managers. About 11.5% are senior managers, while nearly 31% represent C-level leadership and heads of departments. Close to 32% of the leaders surveyed hold more than fifteen years of experience, and the professional experience of close to 47% of the respondent sample spans more than ten years. The ensuing sections will cover the findings and analysis in detail.

Respondent sample

FIGURE 20:

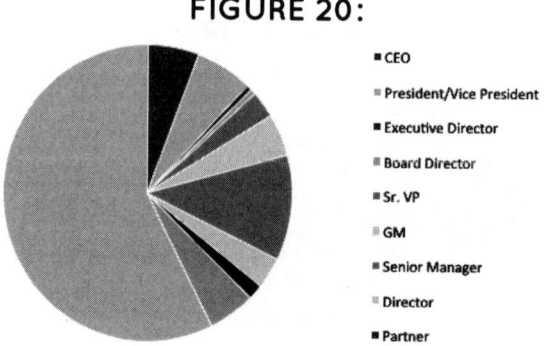

Source: WILL-KPMG's survey on balanced boards, 2013

Respondent sample: education and work experience

1.1.1.1. Educational qualifications

FIGURE 21:

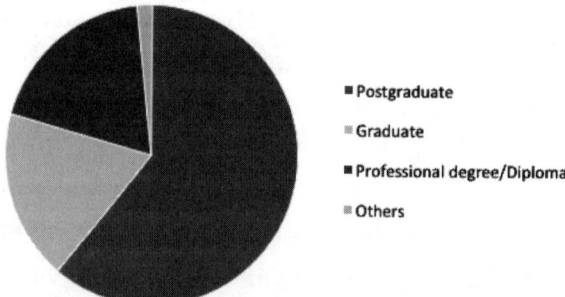

Source: WILL-KPMG's survey on balanced boards, 2013

1.1.1.2 Total work experience

FIGURE 22:

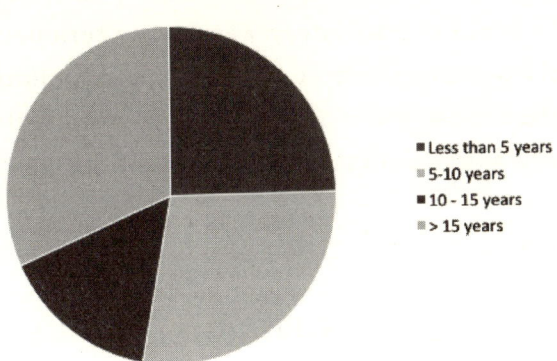

Source: *WILL-KPMG's survey on balanced boards, 2013*

Finding 1: Merit is not given merit in Corporate India

Considering the dynamic and ever-evolving nature of business – establishing balanced leadership and an inclusive leadership framework is becoming core to creating adaptive, innovative and sustaining organisations. Inclusivity and diversity represent important components of a balanced leadership model, which, in turn, constitute the foundations of a successful business and societal organisation. Research indicates that women managers possess unique styles of leadership and skills sets that ultimately augur well in enhancing business performance. Certain traits that are intrinsic in character to women can help organisations enhance a collaborative style of leadership, thereby raising productivity and leadership capability.

India, despite the development it has seen over time, is not as progressive as it really should be. On the one hand, the country exhibits the various elements of advancement that are characteristic of an emerging economic superpower; on the other, it continues to be in cultural slumber as far as its perceptions around women, men and their respective roles are concerned.

Reflecting and reinforcing this thought, most respondents of the 2013 WILL-KPMG survey agree that women in India continue to be at the receiving end of archaic prejudices and a patriarchal mindset. These, they believe, are among the biggest roadblocks to women assuming senior positions on the boards of companies.

While there's no denying that women in India are qualified to assume such important roles (about 76% respondents agree), several other factors take precedence over merit. These include leadership deficit; lack of aspiration and inspiration; absence of networks for women to get nominated to board positions; excessive gender bias; and lack of operational flexibility at the workplace.

FIGURE 23:
What do you think restricts/constrains women from being nominated as members of corporate boards?

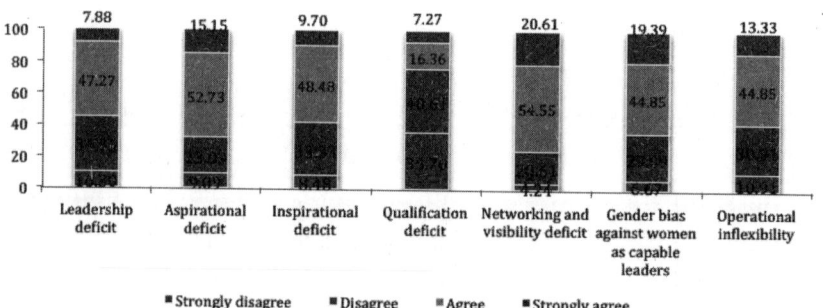

Source: *WILL-KPMG's survey on balanced boards, 2013*

The survey also substantiates the World Economic Forum (WEF)'s alarming findings on the status of women in India. The WEF ranked India at 105 among 135 countries in its Gender Gap Index 2012. This imbalance is reflected in the male-female ratio of company boards, which is a major concern for the survey respondents. About 90% believe that Indian companies fare poorly on gender diversity vis-à-vis other countries due to cultural difference; differences in family roles; and inspirational differences.

Currently, women occupy only fifty-nine of the 1,112 directorships of hundred Indian companies listed on the Bombay Stock Exchange (BSE). Half of these women are independent directors. In 2011, 9.8% directors across the globe were women, and 58.5% companies had at least one woman on their boards. Consequently, according to a study titled 'Board Diversity in India' conducted by the Hyderabad-based Institute of Public Enterprises, India ranks thirty-eighth in the world in terms of women's representation on boards.

Other countries such as Malaysia (ranked hundred on the WEF's Gender Gap Index 2012), Norway (ranked at three), and Australia (ranked twenty-five) have proactively adopted measures to increase gender diversity in company boards. Malaysia aims to

FIGURE 24:

Poor gender diversity in Indian corporate boards vis-à-vis other countries can be attributed to:

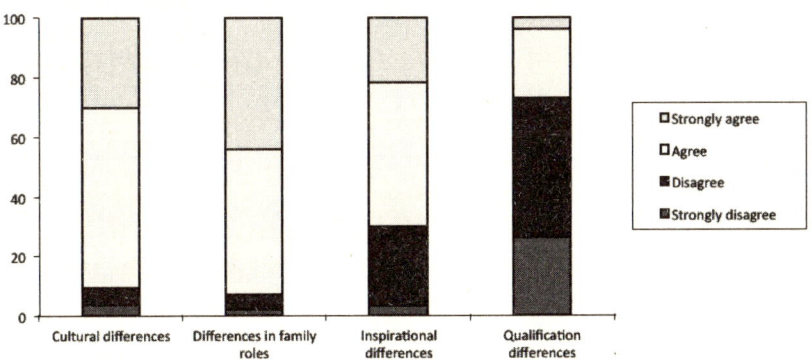

Source: WILL-KPMG's survey on balanced boards, 2013

increase the percentage of women on boards to 30% within five years; Australia has demanded companies to regularly report on gender ratios; and the European Union is considering a legislation that would mandate forty companies to appoint 40% of women on their boards.

Finding 2: Balanced boards enhance leadership effectiveness

Against the backdrop of a constantly evolving economic landscape, the global economic balance has shifted in favour of emerging markets as the developed world struggles to regain its position by boosting growth. Thus, countries are reinventing business strategies; and organisations are reviewing the roles and responsibilities of their professionals to stay afloat in this highly competitive world.

This change has been accompanied by a transformation in the role of women and their aspirations. It is no longer enough for a woman to be only financially independent; instead, it has become equally important to ascend the career trajectory and assume leadership positions to participate in and influence corporate strategies on an equal footing with men.

Some external studies have found a positive correlation between balanced boards and corporate top lines, highlighting the strategic role that balanced governance plays in effective leadership and performance.

According to the WILL-KPMG 2013 survey, *more than 90% of the respondents agree that the increased representation of women at the management level is likely to enhance board leadership effectiveness.* This can be gauged from the efficacy of critical business qualities such as establishing business direction to tap opportunities, managing operations, and strengthening business relations with stakeholders, among others.

FIGURE 25:
The increased representation of women at the leadership level is likely to enhance board leadership effectiveness

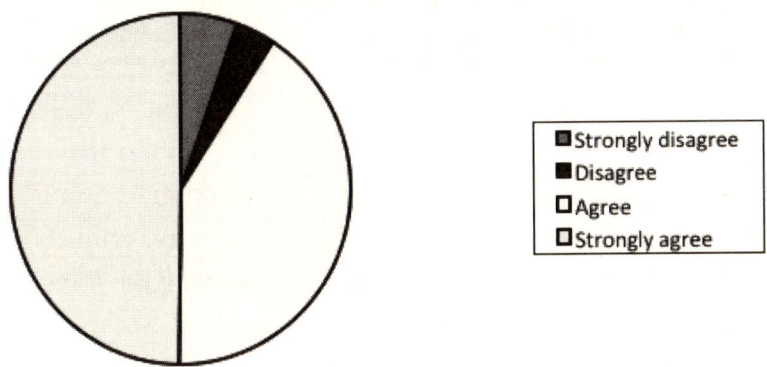

Source: WILL-KPMG's survey on balanced boards, 2013

These overarching qualities may be classified into two broad categories – strategy and business.

Strategy

In the context of strategy, more than 91% of the respondents agree that balanced boards improve decision making, the management of enterprise risk and innovative thinking through diverse perceptions, experiences and management styles. It is commonly believed that men and women follow different approaches to addressing the same problem. About 98% of the respondents believe this "different" perspective is a critical factor in bringing about diversity at the workplace.

FIGURE 26:

'Balanced Boards' are important, as the increased representation of women can generate/augment the following critical business qualities of corporate leadership

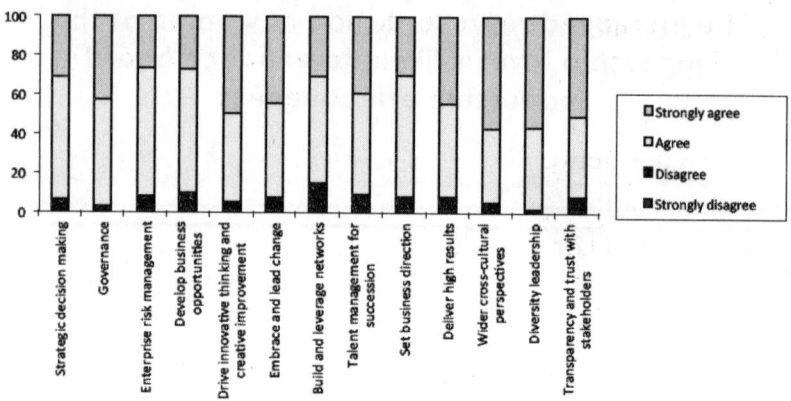

Source: WILL-KPMG's survey on balanced boards, 2013

Business

With respect to business, more than 89% of the respondents share the view that increased numbers of women board members lend direction to the business and development of business opportunities, which enhances financial performance.

This can also be gauged from the survey response, wherein more than 79% of the respondents state that women board members have contributed to increased revenues and reduced costs, leading to profits for their organisations.

Apart from the same technical knowledge and management abilities they share with their male colleagues, women have often been credited with a distinctive set of soft skills that they bring to the table. This combination helps women professionals to effectively forge alliances with stakeholders, colleagues and customers, as well as retain talent. Therefore, more than 90% of the respondents believe that women board members foster productivity – which leads to increased revenues and, consequently, high returns – through their motivational or soft skills. Further, close to 96% are of the view that women employees enhance an organisation's brand image and customer goodwill.

The respondents also believe that women embrace and lead change. However, the only area where they tend to fall short is in leveraging networks. If this shortcoming is overcome, then strategy formation, as well as the growth of business and that of the economy at large, could increase exponentially.

FIGURE 27:

The increased representation of women employees has positively influenced any or all of the following parameters of business performance in your organization

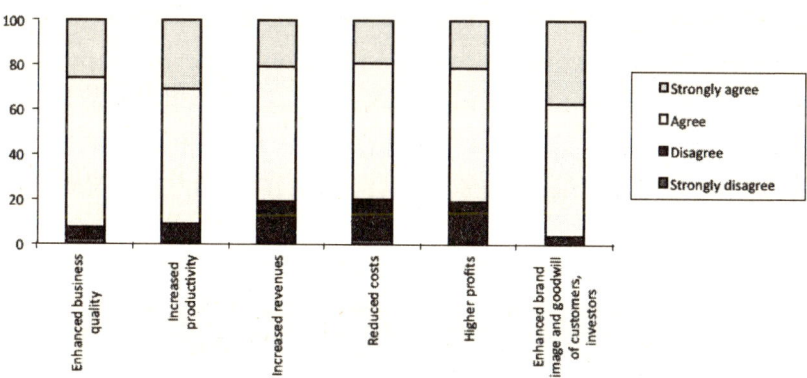

Source: WILL-KPMG's survey on balanced boards, 2013

Finding 3: Balanced boards will improve corporate governance

Balanced boards are considered to be integral to effective corporate governance. The varied perspectives, skills and experiences of both

FIGURE 28:
Balanced boards are integral to effective corporate governance

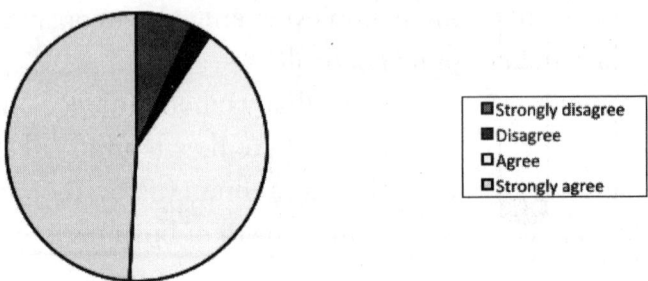

Strongly disagree
Disagree
Agree
Strongly agree

Source: WILL-KPMG's survey on balanced boards, 2013

men and women provide a holistic edge to the agendas of boards, thereby strengthening corporate strategies and decisions. More than 90% of the survey's respondents support this view.

More than 88% of the respondents also agree that women on corporate boards contribute to good governance by improving transparency, facilitating succession planning, evaluating board performance and gaining stakeholder trust. In addition, over 92% of the respondents feel that women tend to be comparatively more

FIGURE 29:

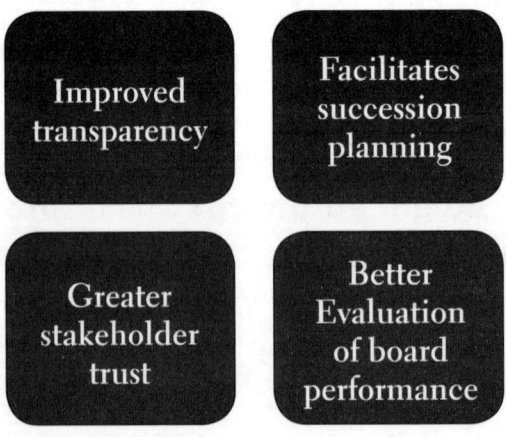

Improved transparency

Facilitates succession planning

Greater stakeholder trust

Better Evaluation of board performance

FIGURE 30:
How Women on corporate boards contribute to good governance

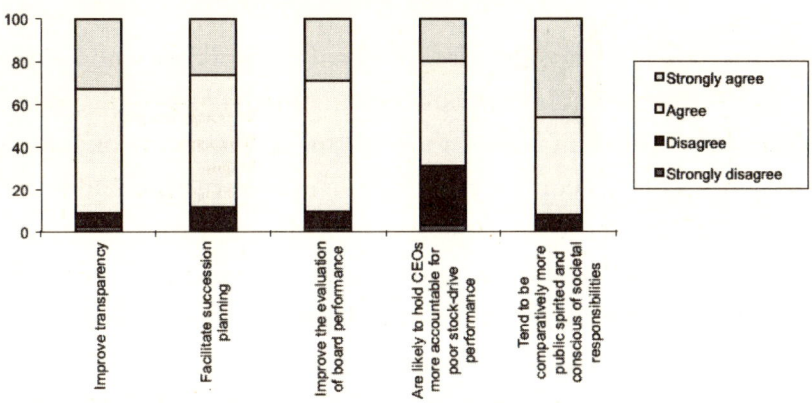

Source: WILL-KPMG's survey on balanced boards, 2013

public spirited and conscious of societal responsibilities, which also facilitates corporate operations and brand building.

Another important aspect of corporate governance is safeguarding shareholder's interests. In this respect, the survey finds that women board members are likely to hold CEOs more accountable than men for poor stock-drive performance – about 70% of our respondents expect this trend. This, in turn, would result in effective risk management – by increasing the scrutiny of all decision-making activities – and ensure high returns.

Balanced boards are not only indicative of increasingly less skewed gender representation. They are also representative of advanced development. Thus, several organisations across industries are expressing increased interest in investing in women employees.

These findings present a strong case for inducting a greater number of women on corporate boards, especially in India, which is a nation of large, qualified, skilled and largely untapped workforce of women.

Finding 4: Initiatives to strengthen balanced leadership are largely compliance-driven and cosmetic in nature

Balanced leadership, gender diversity at the workplace and equal opportunities – such concepts have gained significant ground across enterprises in India in recent times. Yet, most companies across the country continue to function in line with the traditional framework and culture of the Indian corporate world.

It's time to look beyond quotas and compliance – that's the general sentiment of the WILL-KPMG survey's respondents. The majority believe that Indian companies have been taking certain initiatives – such as abiding by regulatory compliances; initiating special leadership training programs for women; and establishing targeted talent-management strategies. However, they also strongly feel that much of this is cosmetic and merely compliance-motivated.

FIGURE 31:

Does your organization have one or all of the following measures to help encourage and support women to advance to corporate leadership from within the organization?

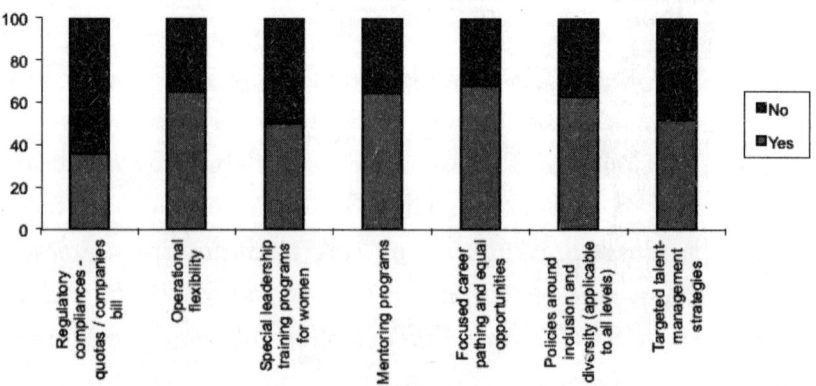

Source: WILL-KPMG's survey on balanced boards, 2013

The need of the hour is to improve operational flexibility and initiate mentoring programs that can prepare women for leadership positions is a sustained and deep-rooted manner – and also gender-sensitivity program for male managers, to help them understand the business imperative of diversity of boards. Moreover, most respondents believe that Indian companies did not have adequate policies on inclusion and diversity across levels.

To address this issue, the survey respondents suggest that companies look beyond simple compliance with women-centric reservations and the Companies Bill 2013 mandate. Instead, companies should acknowledge the contribution of women to business success by increasing their representation in leadership roles; giving impetus to their careers; initiating special mentoring programs to help them be effective with decision making; and providing equal opportunities across levels.

FIGURE 32:

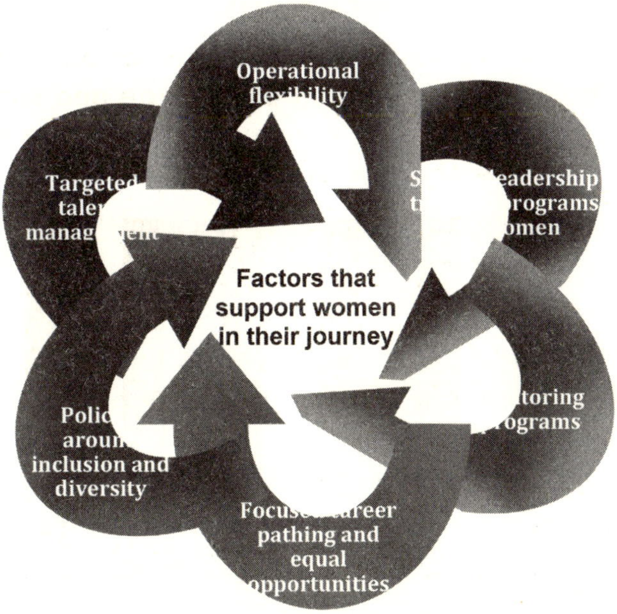

Moreover, about 94% of respondents believe that policies related to inclusion and diversity as well as talent-management strategies for women could support and motivate women to aspire to front-line decision making positions on the corporate ladder.

FIGURE 33:

To encourage and support women to advance to corporate leadership from within, an organization can extend support in the following ways

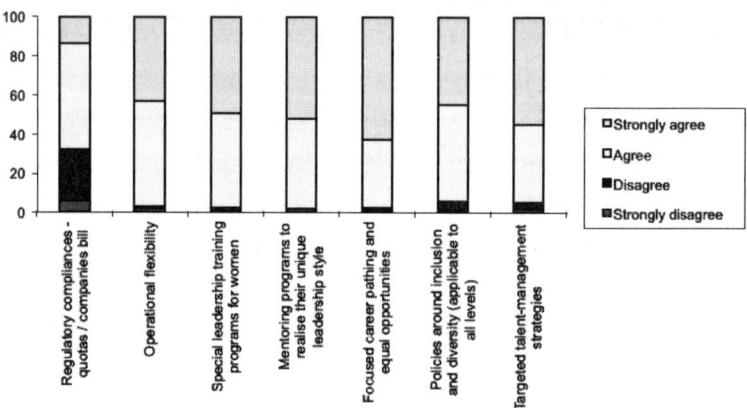

Source: *WILL-KPMG's survey on balanced boards, 2013*

According to the survey respondents, the Companies Bill 2013 – which mandates companies to appoint at least one woman on their boards – may actually increase the likelihood of inappropriate appointments based on family-relatives, spouses, and even mothers of CEOs – being appointed to the board!

In order to rise above mere adherence to norms, companies need to adopt far-reaching and innovative measures. These include the following:

- **Non-mandatory policy of maintaining gender diversity**
  Companies could consider following a non-mandatory policy of maintaining gender diversity and disclosing and elaborating on such measures:

- Management can announce in regular meetings/publications realistic goals towards achieving gender diversity
- Management should define eligibility criteria to identify prospective women board members. Prospective candidates should be trained and mentored so they can perform their duties as leaders to the best of their abilities

- **Special leadership programs for women employees at all levels**
Companies can assist women across the organisational hierarchy to pave career growth and thus ensure low staff turnover and high retention. Companies could also introduce coaching programs for women to help them achieve work-life balance at every stage of their career. Further, relaxations in leave and related policies can facilitate a sense of flexibility at the workplace, which helps women feel valued and allows them to deal with work pressures effectively. Increased pre- and post-maternity leave, sabbaticals, flexible working arrangements during late hours are some potential aids that can support women aspiring to reach the top and also facilitate employee retention.

Closing Remarks on women on Boards

'We must raise both the ceiling and the floor.' – Sheryl Sandberg
In her recent bestseller *Lean In: Women, Work and the Will to Lead*, Facebook COO Sheryl Sandberg advises women professionals to "sit at the table", rise to various challenges, walk the extra mile to achieve their goals and, above all, break the glass ceiling and claim their rightful positions at the top of the corporate order. The popularity of Sandberg's book is not without reason. Over the years, the issue that lies at its heart has transformed into a chronic problem in several countries – including India.

A skewed gender ratio has been slowing down the world's largest democracy for years now. India's performance in several prestigious global assessments on gender equality has been depressingly low – as the country ranked 105th among 135 countries globally in the World Economic Forum's Gender Gap Index 2012. It is, therefore, not surprising that this dismal trend has permeated to almost every aspect of women's lives – and the corporate boardroom is no exception. The representation of women on the boards of several Indian companies (both public and private) currently staggers at a meagre 7% – as compared to Norway, which boasts an astounding 40% of women as board members.

The working women's professional world in India has evolved significantly over time; the winds of change have finally started blowing. – and one can see the direction in which these winds of change are headed.

The interaction with 175 business leaders from leading companies across the country who participated in this survey, reveals that a significant number of companies are increasingly waking up to the fact that the benefits of appointing women board members go way beyond the simple remedying gender imbalance. The majority of the respondents agree that balanced boards are integral to improving company performance, fostering good governance, formulating a positive company image, maintaining a healthy system of checks and balances, and ensuring sustained growth. Moreover, the appointment of women on boards enhances companies' understanding of the consumer base – which is particularly important for the FMCG, finance, retail banking, insurance, consumer and household goods, electronic items, hospitality, healthcare, and several other sectors.

However, neither an individual nor a company can bring about such a change alone and overnight. The process of acknowledging and rewarding women professionals' contributions to a company requires collaboration between various all stakeholders and sustained efforts from senior management and the women themselves. The government plays an important role here. Norway demonstrates that the formulation of women-centric policies is integral to helping women realize their professional ambitions. The Indian Government has seemingly also taken cognizance of this concept, as is evident from its recent legislative decisions. The implementation of the Companies Bill 2013, which mandates every company to appoint at least one woman on their board, is expected to go a long way in creating gender diversity at the senior leadership level.

It is evident from history that a small push from the right quarters can deliver effective results. That's why the need of the hour in this context is to formulate more legislation that supports women professionals and make companies accountable. A suggestion emerging from the survey revolves around providing tax benefits to companies with balanced boards. The survey respondents also believe that certain organisation-level measures could save deserving women from falling by the wayside in their quest to reach the top. These include policies around leave, flexible working arrangements, company forums to address challenges specific to women and help them balance their personal and professional lives.

However, formulating policies accounts for only one half of the solution. It is equally important to ensure their effective implementation.

The concept of "balanced boards has certainly arrived" – as an integral part of good corporate governance for sustainable company growth. Investing in women professionals is not simply a matter of ensuring gender equality, but ensuring that the company is ready and equipped to respond to the promise of innovation, wealth-creation, and best business performance, in smarter and optimized global business formats.

'We need to realize that just making laws and announcing policies would not be enough to empower women. The most fundamental issue is that the mindset of old thoughts of our society have to be changed – giving women equal status as men is a very big challenge and the wall of discrimination has to be demolished.

Women have to be empowered mentally, socially, and financially – for our great country and its citizens to progress in real sense.'

ABOUT THE AUTHOR

Poonam Barua is Founder Director, PAMASIA – an independent firm specializing in corporate and institutional diplomacy, global corporate advisory services, and building leadership across a range of diverse stakeholders, based in New Delhi for almost two decades.

Ms. Barua is also Founder-Chairman of the distinguished *"Forum for Women in Leadership"* and CEO, WILL Forum India – that brings together senior women executives from leading companies in India and multinationals on the mission and mandate for leveraging the vast talent-pool of women, sharing best practices for women in the workplace, and mentoring women for leadership positions. Over 6,000 senior women professionals from across 250 companies, and over 600 WILL Mentees – are participating in the WILL Forum since its launch in 2007, that are redefining "balanced leadership" for future business success and societal stakeholders. Founding members of the WILL Forum India include Tata Consultancy Services, KPMG and Infosys Technologies.

Ms. Barua has authored several WILL Research Reports and surveys on "WILL Handbook: 50-Best Practices for Women in the Workplace," "Differentiating Styles of Women in Leadership," "WILL User's Guide: Mentoring Women for Best Rewards,"

"WILL-KPMG Report: Women and Enterprise Risk Management" and the best selling report "Balanced Boards for Good Governance."

For over a decade, Ms. Barua has been Regional Director – India, The Conference Board, New York, providing thought-leadership on best business practices for top-management, CEO's, HR leaders, and Board Directors. She has also launched the highly successful "Human Resources Council – India" and "Council on Corporate Governance & Risk Management" in India. Ms. Barua is fully committed to bringing transparency and corporate governance to business India, and serves as an independent director on corporate boards, leads the pioneering "WILL Women on Corporate Boards: Series" in India, and is a Member of the Joint Electricity Regulation Commission Advisory Board, of the Indian government.

Ms. Barua has been awarded a Visiting Scholarship at The Wharton School Advanced Management Program for her work on women in leadership. She also holds a Ford Fellowship at the Paul H. Nitze School of Advanced International Studies (SAIS), Johns Hopkins University, for her work on conflict resolution in South Asia. She is a Visiting Fellow at the Henry L. Stimson Center (Washington D.C.) and the Salzburg Seminar in Austria. Ms. Barua has also served as Special Consultant for distinguished international institutions – including the Eisenhower Fellowships, London Business School, Financial Markets International Inc., and East-West Center.

Ms. Barua is a trained economist with a Master's Degree from the prestigious Delhi School of Economics, and has served as Chief Program Specialist for over a decade at the United States Information Service in New Delhi. She has also been a Lecturer in Economics at Delhi University and Research Associate at the Indian Institute of Public Administration.